A BIRD IN THE HAND

Frontispiece Hawking group, Wool Heath 1901.

A BIRD IN THE HAND
Celebrated falconers of the past
by Roger Upton

with a foreword by the Duke of St. Albans
Hereditary Grand Falconer of England

Debretts Peerage Limited

Dedication

The Peregrine

'My friends and I have ever found thee,
And as all who seek shall find thee,
As long as thou art to be found.
Adorned with every good gift —
Beauty, grace, strength, and unmatchable speed,
Courage, skill and perseverance —
To all these dost add the tameness
And docility that so admirably adapts
   thee to be a companion,
Friend, and servant of Man.'

Reminiscences of a Falconer, Major C. Hawkins Fisher

© Roger Upton 1980.

Published by Debrett's Peerage Limited
73/77 Britannia Road, London SW6

ISBN 0 905649 34 6

Book design by Hobson and Whitty
Wilton, Wiltshire

Typeset by Shaun Ryan Typesetting
Bournemouth

Printed in the Netherlands by de Lange/van Leer BV

CONTENTS

Acknowledgements

I would like to thank the following for their help and encouragement in making this book possible:

S. H. Bath, (Photographer) Devon.
Mrs Maureen Black.
Nicky Blundell-Brown.
James Chick.
Gus Cockrill.
Prudence Cumming, (Photographer) London.
Mr & Mrs F. Fisher.
Stephen Frank.
Mr Frost.
Mrs D. Gladstone.
Mr & Mrs Winston F. C. Guest.
Robert Jarman.
Mrs James Robertson-Justice.
Norman Knight.
Lady Mary Legard.
Mr G. F. Lewis.
Alistair Mann.
Douglas Mann.
Mrs J. J. Mann.
Alan Morriss.
Miss Anastasia Noble.
Mark Palmer.
Alan Peters.
Mr & Mrs R. Portman.
Ted Roberts.
Thomas W. Rose, (Photographer) New York.
William Ruttledge.
Candida Spencer.
Thomas-Photos, Oxford.
Peter Upton, (Artist).
Charles Young, (Fine Paintings) London.
Elizabeth Young.
The Greater London Council as Trustees of the Iveagh Bequest.
The British Falconers' Club.

The publishers wish to thank the Trion Gallery Limited for permission to reproduce the paintings by George Lodge.

Foreword
by the Duke of St. Albans O.B.E.

I am delighted that the Publisher of this fascinating book should have seen fit to approach me to write this Foreword. The choice was appropriate enough as for over 300 years the appointment of Hereditary Grand Falconer of England and Master of the King's Hawks has been held by the Dukes of St. Albans. It was originally Charles II who appointed his son, the first Duke of St. Albans, to the post, which, happily for my ancestors, remained a lucrative one until the last century.

Roger Upton is well known to me, not only as a practising falconer but also for his knowledge of the history of the sport and as one of its foremost champions. I would especially mention the leading role he played in the most successful international conference on falconry held in Abu-Dhabi in 1976, under the Chairmanship of His Excellency Sheikh Sultan bin Zayid al Nihayyan, when falconers from all over the world enjoyed the hospitality of that great falconer and patron of falconers, His Highness Sheikh Zayid bin Sultan al Nihayyan, Ruler of Abu Dhabi, President of the United Arab Emirates.

It is perhaps hard for us today to understand the part that falconry used to play in people's lives and it's importance to them. As a sport in the Middle Ages its popularity and the number of its followers could perhaps be compared to those of football in the modern world. It was practised with passion by all from the Emperor to the humblest in the land. However, falconry was not just a sport it was also perhaps the most effective means of replenishing the larder. The arrival of gunpowder was to change all this, as indeed it did for the bow and arrow. The relevance of falconry today in this atomic and computerised age must be different. To me it lies in the enduring basis of the sport, that is the relationship that man must establish with a wild creature in an element which is not his own, and to do so with no technological aides that were not available to him a thousand years ago.

In this book Roger Upton has documented those famous falconers who kept the sport alive after it had waned in popularity and has shown how their dedication resulted in the sport reaching levels of quality which have not since been equalled. Although not a practising falconer, I have always maintained a very great interest in the sport and the greatest admiration for its practitioners. I am delighted at the publication of this volume which so magnificently documents some of our greatest falconers and explains the very special relationship which they had with each other and with their hawks.

St. Albans, February 1980

The Seal of the Hereditary Grand Falconer of England.

Introduction

This book is about a few famous falconers of the past, men who enjoyed the flight of a falcon, and who, by their pursuit of the old art, helped to keep it alive, just as those of us who follow the sport today will keep its skills, secrets and pleasures safe for those who follow us. I do not claim to have included all the 'Celebrated Falconers of the Past', nor do I suggest that those that I have included are necessarily the *most* celebrated, but at least all of them pursued the sport with energy, enthusiasm and love.

Of necessity much of what I have written has been gleaned from other books. Fortunately many falconers made comments in the margins of their falconry books. Some kept beautiful diaries, often profuse in their comments on good days, short and to the point on other pages. Others wrote articles, notes and letters to friends with reports on their sport or with advice to beginners. From these varied sources I have tried to glean some history, some useful hints and ideas from past masters, and to report on past falconers' successes in the field.

It will, I hope, make interesting reading for those who appreciate the fascination of falconry.

For those who read this book and do not know anything of falconry the following notes may be of help.

Falconry is the pursuit of wild quarry, in its natural surroundings, with trained hawks. These hawks may be of many species but largely fall into two main types, long-winged hawks, dark of eye, such as the peregrine, gyr or merlin, and short-winged yellow-eyed hawks, such as the goshawk or sparrowhawk.

The short-winged hawks are normally flown directly from the hand at their quarry. Reckless, active and brave hawks, they will fly many times in a day, pursuing their quarry with a short sharp dash and often killing deep in cover, tangled in bush or brambles. The goshawk will take rabbits, coots, moorhens, pheasants, the occasional partridge and a good female will sometimes take a hare. The sparrowhawk is flown at the blackbird or thrush; females may also take partridge or moorhen. The tiny male sparrowhawk is properly called a 'musket'.

The long-winged hawks are of the open country. Some are flown from the fist as are the merlins, when flown at the skylark. Lark hawking demands open country and in such country produces the very finest sport, often with a tiny 'jack', barely ten inches long, climbing up and up to try and best a boldly singing lark.

Rook or seagull hawks, peregrine falcons (meaning females) or tiercels, the correct name for the male peregrine, are also slipped directly from the fist at the quarry, again in open country. Both rooks and seagulls are a difficult quarry to take well and regularly, not perhaps in the autumn but in the wild winter and spring weather.

Peregrines can also be flown 'waiting on' for game or wildfowl. The hawk is encouraged to circle overhead, patiently waiting on, in expectation of quarry being flushed by dogs or falconer below. Game hawking is certainly the most complex and artificial of flights but provides the setting for the downright, headlong, dramatic stoop from many hundreds of feet at an active and tough quarry, good to eat for both falcon and falconer.

The language of hawking has added some words to our present day vocabulary. A hawk rarely drinks but occasionally sips water when it is said to 'bowse', an old hawk is known as a 'haggard', and when many hawks are needed in the field they are carried on a 'cadge' by the 'cadger'.

But much of the specialist language has fallen into disuse, even by the modern day falconer. Rarely do you hear a hawk's wings properly called her 'sails' or her tail her 'train'. Her breast feathers are correctly called her 'mail' and her home the 'mews', now more often called the hawk house.

The equipment used by falconers has altered little since the time of Colonel Thornton, the subject of the first chapter in this book. We still use a hood, although most practical falconers now find the lighter hoods, adapted from the Indian patterns, more convenient and pleasant for the hawk than the heavy ornate hoods of the past. Jesses, the short leather straps attached to the legs, have their variations, but serve the same purpose and some now use nylon instead of leather for a leash.

In quotes from falconers' diaries and in captions to the photographs some technical terms have of necessity been used. I therefore include a short simple glossary which appears on p 157.

One successful falconer once wrote that good falconry was the finest sport in the world, bad falconry the very worst. As with all arts, falconry is better practised by those who do it well, those who have the gift of understanding what is falconry. It is not for those who would make an exhibition of it or turn it to commercial gain. It is a fine field sport and only for those dedicated enough to do it justice, despite the difficulties of achieving real and continued success in the field. For that is where the skills and competence of a falconer are to be judged.

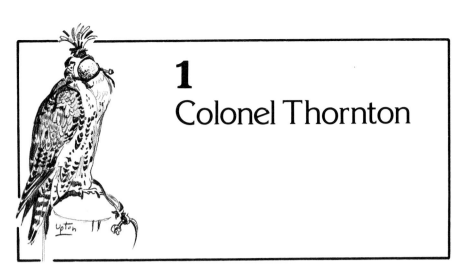

1
Colonel Thornton

What are the qualifications needed to become a successful falconer? Of course a knowledge of the training, flying and daily management of birds of prey is necessary, but to be a celebrated falconer more is needed. If we study the writings of Emperor Frederick II of Hohenstaufen we will find that 'The falconer should be of a medium size; if he is too tall he is likely to be easily tired and not nimble; on the other hand, if he is too small his movements, either on horseback or on foot, may be too quick and sudden. He ought to be moderately fleshy, so that he is not handicapped by emaciation and thus be unable to do hard work or to withstand the cold; nor should he be so fat that he is likely to shun exertion and suffer from the heat. The falconer must not be one who belittles his art and dislikes the labour involved in his calling. He must be diligent and persevering, so much so that as old age approaches he will still pursue the sport out of pure love of it. For, as the cultivation of an art is long and new methods are constantly introduced, a man should never desist in his efforts but persist in its practise while he lives, so that he may bring the art itself nearer to perfection.'

Perhaps it is hardly surprising that so few become falconers. To live up to such standards must be beyond most of us, but many of these qualifications are indeed necessary, particularly a fanatical love of the sport. This the celebrated falconers had to a high degree.

Let us start with one such — Colonel Thomas Thornton of Thornville Royal in Yorkshire. Born in 1757, the estates and wealth of the family became his on the early death of his father, Colonel William Thornton, in 1771. Young Thomas Thornton, educated at Charterhouse and later at Glasgow College, early developed a passion for all sports, and for field sports in particular. Requiring a larger and more impressive home than the family seat, Old Thornville, it is said that he paid the Duke of York £110,000 for the property that became known as Thornville Royal. There he created a sporting paradise that became famous in the annals of falconry, hunting and shooting. He kept a pack of foxhounds and a pack of beagles. He owned a large kennel of coursing greyhounds and a particularly famous kennel of pointers. Always an experimenter, Thornton was the first to cross a foxhound with a pointer, and produced a dog of outstanding excellence, Sydenham Edwards writing that '[Thornton] has improved the breed by selecting the lightest and gayest

Colonel Thomas Thornton

From a Painting by Reinagle.   *Facing page 310.*

individuals, and, by judicious crosses with the foxhound, to procure courage and fleetness'.

Hawks were kept on a vast scale and the Colonel pursued his sport over all the surrounding country — Grassington and Blubberhouses, Clifford and Bramham moor and a fine heronry at Bailby Grange. What more could a falconer want? Yet when the crops were standing the Colonel removed to the Yorkshire wolds, then all grass, and twelve miles from Scarborough, at Boythorpe, he built a lodge called Falconer's Hall.

He was also 'proposer and manager' of the Confederate Hawks of Great Britain, more commonly known as the Falconers' Club, from 1772 until 1781. The headquarters of this Club was at Bourn Bridge, Cambridgeshire, during the month of March for kite and crow hawking; then in April and May they hawked near Barton Mills and Brandon in Suffolk. The hawks went out on Saturdays, Mondays and Wednesdays. In 1783, when the Club was under the management of the Earl of Orford, the cadge consisted of thirty-two slight falcons (peregrines), thirteen German hawks (presumed to be goshawks) and seven Iceland falcons.

The early writers suggested that a falconer should be active and healthy. Colonel Thornton, for a wager, once walked four miles in thirty-two minutes and on another occasion jumped six five-barred gates in six minutes, then mounted a horse and repeated the exercise.

In 1786 he set out on a sporting tour of Scotland. A sloop, the *Falcon*, was chartered in London. Stores, including two boats named the *Ville de Paris* and the *Gibraltar*, were embarked, as were servants, guns, dogs and nets. The crew consisted of the Captain, two mariners, the falconer, waggoner, groom and boy.

On **24 July**, William Lawson, head falconer and inspector-general, reported on the examination of stores and livestock: *Ham, bacon, reindeer and other tongues, smoked beef, pigs' countenances etc., enough to serve till the end of October. Pickles, sweetmeats etc., ditto biscuits, damaged. Tents and tent equipage, nets of all kinds, pegs for the tents, wanting. Oatmeal, wanting.*

Hawks in good order: 'Miss M'Gee' *and* 'Miss L. Townsend', *red falcons, and* 'Death' *and* 'Devil', *red tiercels. Hawks in bad order:* 'Croc Franc' *and* 'Craigon', *red tiercels.*

Setters: Pero, Cato, Claret *and* Sancho *(lame).*

Pointers: Carlo, Dargo, Sappho, Pero, Dash, Pluto.

Deer Hound: Orson.

All in good order.

Guns all in good order: two double barrels, one rifle, three single barrels.

Gunpowder: Powder dry, 40 lbs. Ditto rather damp, 40 lbs.

Shot, eleven bags. Flints sufficient.

Two wagons to go off tomorrow to Inverness for oatmeal, corn, groceries, and other household articles, wines, etc.

In 1804 Thornton's book entitled **A Sporting Tour through the Northern Parts of England and great part of the Highlands of Scotland** was published. Most unkindly reviewed by Sir Walter Scott, it nevertheless remains a fascinating report of the difficulties and problems of organizing such an expedition and, even allowing for Thornton's tendency to exaggeration, it shows the sporting potential of the Highlands before they became a place of yearly pilgrimage. Hawking

Young tiercel at hack

Young tiercel and falcon just after being taken up from hack

mainly snipe and duck, Thornton also tried the hawks at grouse and ptarmigan with success. The freedom to fish, shoot or hawk where or at what he wished and the hospitality of the landowners ensured success. Hawks were first flown on 24 July and entered to grey plover. On the 26th they again flew well but the Colonel had one setback with the discovery that Claret *(procured as an addition to the pointers I had, and brought to Raits with infinite care and trouble)* was really good for nothing, and though much pains were taken to reclaim him, he proved of no use.

By **4 August** the hawks were taking snipe. Sheer fatigue, perhaps, gave rise to some exaggeration, for once on mountains in Glen Eunach, the highest hill being about 4,200 feet, Thornton writes: *Let the reader figure to himself a mountain at least 18,000 feet above him, and a steep precipice of 13,000 feet below, encompassed with conical and angular rocks; then let him imagine men and horses scrambling over huge masses of stone, which, though of immense size, are frequently loose, and at every step seem as if the next would carry them off into the air beyond its edges, and the very idea will be enough to make him shudder. Yet the eye, having dwelt awhile on these frightful, naked piles, is soon relieved, and feels an agreeable composure from the scene beneath, where the lake, like a sheet of glass, reflects, on its extensive bosom, all the objects around: this, bordered by soft, sandy banks, whose fine but partial verdure, scattered over with small herds of cattle, grazing and bleating; and a single bothie, the temporary residence of the lonely herdsman, softens, in some measure, the unpleasant idea of danger which is apt to arise; while the solemn silence, interrupted only by the hoarse notes of ptarmigans, increasing at the approach of strangers, or by the dashing of the never-ceasing cascades, soothes the mind with the most agreeable emotions.*

It took five hours for his companions to join him and so exhausted

Falcon and snipe

were they that Captain Waller asked to be left, he was so fatigued. *A thought struck me; I placed a ptarmigan (shot earlier) in such a position that it appeared to be alive, and then mentioning to the Captain that I had seen one, which he never had, immediately on discovering it, he fired and shot it; this revived him more than anything I could have given him. Having shot a ptarmigan was now the only topic of conversation, and it would have been cruel to have undeceived him. Our dinner, which was soon dressed, proved an excellent one; the chief dish consisted of two brace and a half of ptarmigans and a moor-cock, a quarter of a pound of butter, some slices of Yorkshire-smoked ham, and reindeer's tongue; with some sweet herbs, pepper, etc, prepared by the housekeeper at Raits. These, with a due proportion of water, made each of us a plate of very strong soup, which was relished with a keenness of appetite that none but those who have been at Glen Eunach can experience; an appetite, far, very far superior to the pallid one with which the gentlemen at Weltgie's or Lethellier's eat their sumptuous and costly meals.*

Washed down with a bumper of champagne (gentlemen and servants together) they were enabled to proceed.

On **13 August** the hawks killed a brace and a half of wild duck. *One of these flights could not be less than six or eight miles; the duck, which proved to be an old mallard, took the air, and went almost out of sight, but was so hard pressed by both of the falcons that she came out of the air like a shot, and attempted to take refuge in the splash; but, being prevented, she was flushed and raked.*

16 August: *Saw several broods of ptarmigans; the tiercels killed three brace and a half. They were much frightened at the hawks, which they must sometimes see, and their defence we found was, when pressed, to fly under the large loose rocks; so that we found some difficulty to retrieve them.*

On **18 July** Thornton was given a gift by the Laird of Rothemurcos, an eyass goshawk, still in down. As Thornton writes: *The forest, formed by Glenmore and Rothemurcos, I have before observed, produces some noble fir-trees, and is an asylum for stags and roebucks; in it are some eyries of goss-hawks, some of which we saw. (When I managed the Confederate Hawks of England, I always got them from Germany.)*

This hawk is very rare: I never met with any in England that were wild; they are a short-winged hawk, being in the same proportion to a sparrow-hawk (of which kind they are) as a falcon is to a merlin.

They fly at the bolt, and the falcon is excellent for hares, rabbits, herns, and wild ducks; the tiercel for game.

On **27 August** Thornton dedicated the day to public hawking, 'the amusement being little known here'. The hawks killed four and a half brace of grouse which might have been more had they not lost one of the tiercels for some time.

31 August: *The goshawk was lost from the perch with her leash. Not belled, because as yet she had not been flown, there seemed little chance of recovering her.*

3 September: *Messrs Fleming and Monteith, of Barochan Castle, arrived. They brought with them an ample supply of fresh limes, lemons, and China oranges, with marmalade, currant jelly and all kinds of confectionery.*

Still later Thornton reports that: *The Duke of Gordon still keeps up the diversion of falconry, and has several fine hawks of the peregrine and gentle falcon species, which breed in the rocks of Glenmore. I also saw here a true Highland greyhound, which is now become very scarce. It was of a large size, strong, deep-chested, and covered with very long and rough hair. This kind was in great vogue in former days, and used in vast numbers at the magnificent stag-chases by the powerful chieftains.*

Finally returning south, Thornton had dinner with an old friend and

Mallard being pressed by two falcons

Falcon and ptarmigan

15

fellow member of the Falconers' Club, Mr Parker of Marshfield near Settle, and after dinner spent the remainder of the day most happily recounting various flights they had enjoyed at kites, heron and hare at Alconbury Hill and Newmarket.

In 1802 Thornton made another sporting tour, this time through France. Then in 1805 he suddenly sold Thornville Royal, the house, park, gardens and estate to Lord Stourton, for a total of £226,450, with vacant possession January, 1806.

In 1808 Colonel Thornton left Yorkshire for the open downland of Wiltshire. He took a lease on Spye Park and moved his goods and chattels with as much ceremony and pomp as he did most things: falconers dressed in green and silver in charge of many species of hawks, keepers in the Thornton livery leading the famous pointers and gundogs, hunt staff in charge of one hundred couple of foxhounds, otterhounds, beagles and staghounds and a cartload of terriers, thoroughbred horses, rugged in deerskins, a wagonload of luggage piled with guns, rods, hawking poles, otter spears and skins of stag and roe, cormorants trained for fishing, wild boar, and many waggons loaded with red deer, roe, ducks, ferrets, works of art, and a further nine waggons of vintage wines and ales.

While at Spye, Thornton attempted to fly his hawks at the great bustard, then still found on Salisbury Plain and Black Heath, but the hawks found them beyond their powers and their speed too great despite their apparent slowness.

In about 1815 Colonel Thornton gave up hawking and left England for France. He purchased the château of Pont le Roi, Département d'Aube, selling it again in 1821 to Monsieur Casimir Perier. He then leased a château at Chambord from the Princesse de Wagram. Hounded now by creditors, it seems unlikely that he ever paid for Pont le Roi and in 1819 much of his fine collection of paintings was sold. Using the assumed title of the Marquis de Pont he lived on in France until his death in Paris in 1823.

No doubt Thornton was an extraordinary man. Given to extreme exaggeration, he was a man of many enemies one of whom said of him, 'No man who knew him ever spoke well of him.' He was nevertheless a true eccentric, popular with some, and a fanatical sportsman. A man of humour, even in late life, he found amusement from a newspaper report of his death some two years too early: *I find by the papers that I died after a short illness, much lamented, etc, etc at Paris. However that may be I gave a dinner yesterday to a dozen sportsmen. We had roast beef, plum pudding, Yorkshire goose-pie, and sat up singing most gaily till two this morning. At twelve we had two broiled fowls, gizzards etc, and finished a bottle of old rum in punch. No intoxication, for I went to bed well, and never rose better.*

That he was a falconer of enthusiasm and ability there is no doubt. Using both wild-taken and eyass hawks, employing both Dutch and English falconers, he brought falconry to an excellence, in particular the last of the kite hawking, for which he earned the well-deserved gratitude of his Falconers' Club friends.

Malcolm Fleming of Barochan Towers,
Renfrewshire

2
Edward Newcome and The Loo Club

A good friend of Colonel Thornton was Malcolm Fleming of Barochan Castle, near Paisley, in Renfrewshire. While Thornton was on his grand tour of the Highlands of Scotland, Fleming joined him to enjoy the hawking, for Fleming came of a family famous for generations as falconers of renown. At the end of the fifteenth century, an ancestor, Peter Fleming, was presented with a jewelled hawk hood by James IV of Scotland as a memorial of a tiercel of Fleming's beating the King's falcon in a flight at quarry.

Malcolm Fleming kept the Renfrewshire Subscription Hawks at Barochan until his death in 1819. There the hawks were flown at partridges and woodcock. John Anderson was head falconer, with George Harvey as assistant falconer until 1818, when Peter Ballantyne joined Anderson. Together they continued to work for the Renfrewshire Subscription Hawks until 1832. After the death of Fleming the Club continued under the able management of Sir John Maxwell of Pollack, the hawks staying at Barochan. The Club was enthusiastically supported by many local sportsmen, one such being Mr Wallace of Kelly, at one time M.P. for Greenock. After the closure of the Subscription Hawks and the retirement of John Anderson, Sir John Maxwell engaged William Barr Junior as his private falconer in 1845. Barr's father, William Barr Senior had been Sir John's gamekeeper and falconer when Anderson had been at Barochan. At the coronation of George IV in 1820, John Anderson was there to represent the Duke of Atholl. He presented the King with a 'cast' of peregrines, that being the feudal tenure by which the Duke of Atholl held the Isle of Man from the Crown.

The original oil painting, by J. Howe of Edinburgh, commissioned in 1811, shows Malcolm Fleming on horseback. John Anderson stands with a cast of tiercels on his fist, feeding one up on a partridge, which, judging from the pleased expression on the face of Anderson, the tiercel had just killed. Seated is the assistant falconer, George Harvey, with another cast of peregrines. Four spaniels, looking just as pleased as the falconer, watch the hawks, and a handsome pointer takes little notice of his master, who has with him a favourite black poodle.

George, Earl of Orford, President of the Confederate Hawks of Great Britain, apparently started the Club in about 1770. In 1772, Colonel Thornton became manager of the Club and so continued for nine

Edward Clough Newcome

(*opposite*) A Peregrine Falcon: Oil painting, English school; provenance – The Earls of Berkeley, Berkeley Castle.

Kite Hawking. An oil painting by Joseph Wolf, painted in 1856. This fine picture shows two gryfalcons at a kite.

(opposite) A peregrine falcon belonging to the Confederate Hawks of Great Britain at Didlington, Norfolk 1831
(from a painting by Sir Edwin Landseer)

seasons. After this the Earl again took over the running of the Club until his death in 1792. The Club was maintained on a princely scale, for crow, kite and heron hawking. Passage falcons taken at Valkenswaard, Holland, were used with some gyrfalcons, and Dutch falconers were employed. The membership of the Club in 1781 stood at fifty-five and boasted a Club chaplain in the suitably named Mr Edward Parsons. It is certain that the Fleming family in Scotland, and Thornton, Lord Orford and later Lord Berners in England, kept the old sport alive through a period when it had but a small following.

On Lord Orford's death, the Club passed into the management of Major Wilson of Didlington Hall. Major Wilson later became Lord Berners, of the same family as Dame Juliana Berners, Abbess of Sopwell, who wrote **The Boke of St Albans** in 1486, the earliest printed book which relates to falconry. As with the Flemings so does the sport crop up again and again in the same families.

The hawks were kept at High Ash, near Major Wilson's home and the principal quarry was heron, kites having become scarce.

The professional falconers were Dutchmen, James Bots being Master Falconer. John Pells was also with them for some time. Pells came to England in about 1800 and for a while divided his time between heron hawking with the Club in the spring and early summer, and game hawking with John Hall of Cambridgeshire in the autumn of each year.

Heron hawking took place during May and June and was extremely popular, often as many as 150 people turning out to see the sport. The hawking must have been of the highest quality, for in 1822 the Club hawks took a total of 173 herons. Most of these would be saved alive and,

'Box' cadge of fresh-caught passage peregrines.

before being released, would be ringed on the leg with a brass tag marked 'Major Wilson — Didlington Hall' and the date. From recoveries of these birds something was learnt of the habits and longevity of herons. On occasion some were recaught in Holland.

The heronry at Didlington in Norfolk was carefully preserved for the hawking, but the drainage of the fens and the enclosure of much of the open heath over which the falconers followed their hawks made the continuation of heron hawking on any scale very difficult and on Lord Berners' death in 1838 the Falconers' Club ended after maintaining the traditions of heron and kite hawking in England for nearly seventy years.

For many years English falconers had relied on the hawk trappers of Valkenswaard for the passage or haggard falcons used in heron hawking and had employed professional falconers from there. It occurred to some members of the old Club that they might do better to take themselves to Holland where herons were aplenty than bring both falcons and falconers to England where their quarry had become so scarce. So the Loo Club came into being. The majority of members were from England and the Club was under the management of Edward Clough Newcome of Feltwell, Hockwold, in Norfolk.

Edward Clough Newcome, born in 1810, first became involved in falconry when, as a young man, he used to go out with the heron hawks at Didlington at the invitation of Colonel Wilson. According to the wind direction, so would the hawks meet at High Ash, Methwold, Northwold, Mundford or Cranwich Barn, the last being the best place for a high ringing flight. Meeting in the evening, the falconers gathered downwind of the Didlington heronry and there intercepted the herons returning from distant feeding on rivers, ponds and marshes. Then was heron hawking at its finest with the herons intent on reaching safety at the heronry, climbing upwards into the wind and ringing to make height from which they could dive for the safety of the trees.

In the summer of 1839 two members of the old Club went to Holland and at Het Loo, with twenty-one falcons and three falconers – Jan Bots, Arnold Bots and Jan van den Boom – 140 herons were taken. From this the Loo Hawking Club developed, under the presidency of His Royal Highness Prince Alexander of the Netherlands. Among its thirty or so members were the Prince of Orange, Prince Frederick and Prince Henry of the Netherlands, the Duke of Leeds, Lord Hamilton, Lord Strathmore and of course, Edward Newcome. Two groups of falconers were organized under the head falconers, Jan Bots and Adrian Mollen, with up to twenty or so falcons to each group.

The fortunes of the Club varied from season to season but huge numbers of heron were taken. In 1841 287 were taken, there being forty-four falcons in the mews. In 1852 a team of thirty-six falcons took a total of 297. In 1850 the King of Holland maintained, at his own expense, a separate unit under Adrian Mollen and two assistant falconers. The Club employed Jan Bots and his two under-falconers and were responsible for the Club horses.

In August, 1839, eager to try the Arctic gyrfalcons at heron, Newcome travelled to Dovrefeld in Norway. Within three weeks he captured three passage gyrs, a female and two males, and in 1842 the management of the

(opposite) 'Sultan' , a passage falcon; from an oil painting by Sonderland. The property of Edward Clough Newcome, this falcon was famous as a heron hawk, flown in a cast with 'De Ruyter' during the 1840s.

Loo Club sent Jan Bots and Jan van den Boom to Dovrefeld for the same purpose. They caught nine gyrfalcons in a month. While trapping the Dutchmen found remains of old trapping huts used many years earlier. In 1776 Master Falconer Jacques Verhoeven of Denmark had applied for permission for Lord Orford and the Dutch falconer, François Becker, to be allowed to capture gyrfalcons in Norway. Few of these gyrfalcons turned out to be good heron hawks and those that were, being so much more powerful and hard-stooping than the peregrine, damaged the herons or indeed killed them, which did not help the careful management of the heronry.

The Loo Hawking Club continued heron hawking until 1853 and well upheld the standards and excellence of its predecessor at Didlington. Everything was in favour of success: an almost unlimited supply of fresh-taken passage peregrines, excellent falconers conversant with heron hawking and with generations of experience behind them, and above all perfect country for hawking at heron: a vast heath, suitable for riding over, stretching for miles and miles and, isolated in this vast area, a wood containing a very large heronry numbering several thousand pairs of heron. To feed, the herons had to fly perhaps fifteen to twenty miles to the Zuiderzee, giving many opportunities for flights to the falconers waiting downwind of the heronry. Two parties of falconers were usually out, mounted, with a cast of falcons ready, spare falcons on the cadge in charge of an assistant.

Perhaps five or ten miles from the heronry, the falconers would watch for a heron returning from feeding; then, letting it pass on upwind of them, they would cast off one falcon or more, usually a 'cast' or pair of peregrines that flew well together. The heron, already high, would strive to stay above the peregrines all the while edging toward the shelter of the heronry, perhaps casting up the fish, frog or eel from its crop to reduce weight. Meanwhile the hawks would start ringing up in huge circles endeavouring to get above the heron. Higher and higher the three would climb, all the time drifting with the wind, with falconers and followers riding hard to keep the flight in view. If good enough, the falcons would eventually get above the heron, all three now probably tiny dots in the sky. Then the hawks would stoop in turn, driving the heron lower and lower as it lost height evading the repeated stoops. Perhaps one falcon would bind to a wing or deliver a particularly telling blow and soon heron and hawks would come down in a flurry of wings and feathers. On the ground the heron could be a danger to the falcons, using its beak as a spear, so falconers rode fast to be in time to take up their falcons and secure the heron alive. After careful examination for any injury, the heron would be ringed as had been done at Didlington, then released, but only after the long black feathers were drawn from the heron's neck to be kept as a trophy. These were usually presented to the first gentleman or lady rider to come up, who would wear them, pinned with jewels in a velvet cap. Such was heron hawking.

The Club, after twelve glorious seasons, came to an end in 1853. The Royal patronage was withdrawn and heron hawking was reduced to the single efforts of that most skilful and experienced gentleman falconer, Edward Clough Newcome. For ten years, until the formation of the Old

(opposite) Captain Francis Henry Salvin, falconer and cormorant trainer

The Rev Gage Earle Freeman

(opposite) 'The Princess', 1864. A favourite falcon belonging to Gage Earle Freeman

Hawking Club, he was the backbone of what little falconry there was in England. Still heron hawking, but not always able to procure fresh-taken passage hawks from Holland, he successfully tried eyass falcons at heron. Two eyass falcons, 'Verbaea' and 'Vengeance', took several herons in the spring of 1854.

Rook hawking now began to occupy much of his time and he succeeded in encouraging rooks to nest near his home. Stone curlews also afforded some sport and he had varying success with merlins at larks. Game hawking he thought little of, far preferring the ringing flights of peregrines at herons, or rooks and merlins at skylarks. No falconer ever did more to keep alive the ancient sport and great was his encouragement to aspiring falconers.

One enthusiastic member of the Loo Hawking Club was the Duke of Leeds. Well before the formation of that club the Duke, then the Marquess of Carmarthen, kept a large mews of hawks, both passengers and eyasses, his falconer being John Pells. The Marquess lived at Dunottar House, Stonehaven, in Kincardineshire, and had great success at game hawking, flying at grouse, partridge and woodcock. In the eighteen-thirties, with a team of four peregrines, two tiercels, 'The General' and 'Macduff', and two falcons, 'Pearl' and 'Diamond', each hawk took over sixty partridge and their total score, including grouse and woodcock, came to 316 head.

In the autumn of 1845 the Duke of Leeds sent Pells to Iceland to capture gyrfalcons. The Duke gave eight of the fifteen that Pells brought back to the Loo Club to be entered to heron, but they were not particularly successful, the best being a jerkin named 'Morok'. This hawk took herons quite well but could not be trusted to fly in a cast with another hawk, as he would spend all his time trying to catch his partner. Once lost when flying at heron near the home of Edward Newcome, 'Morok' was taken up safe at the Loo in Holland. There the falconers were exercising the Club falcons and, seeing the jerkin coming up, they took him down and sent word to England that he was safe. Some of the seven gyrs kept by the Duke of Leeds were entered to hares at which they had some little success.

Two other falconers also did much at this time to encourage falconry: the well-known authors on hawking matters, Captain Francis Henry Salvin and the Rev Gage Earl Freeman, M.A. Captain Salvin, with his co-author William Brodrick, was responsible for the production of one of the finest books ever published on the sport, **Falconry in the British Isles**. Salvin, a lifelong falconer, flew hawks in many parts of the country and at all types of quarry. In 1857 he enjoyed a sporting tour of Ireland, with John Barr as his falconer. Travelling through the counties of Cork, Kildare and Tipperary during the months of August, September, October and November, they flew falcons at rooks and tiercels at magpies. Two eyass tiercels, 'Dhuleep Singh' and 'The O'Donohue', took 184 magpies in that time, and three eyass falcons, 'Azrael', 'Assegai' and 'Hydra', took sixty-eight rooks.

Equally clever with the short-winged hawks, Salvin was very successful with male goshawks at pheasant and had a fine female goshawk in 'The Bushman', who excelled at taking hares. Captain Salvin also trained

'Islay', a peregrine falcon, named after her birthplace. Property of Gage Earle Freeman

cormorants to catch trout, a mode of fishing which caused much amusement for himself and his friends. His introduction to this sport came in July, 1846 when Edward Newcome brought a trained cormorant back from Holland. The following summer Salvin also obtained one from Holland which, after much careful training, became most successful and was named 'Isaac Walton'.

The Rev Gage Earl Freeman wrote under the nom de plume of 'Peregrine' in **The Field,** and, as joint author with Captain Salvin of **Falconry — Its Claims, History and Practise** (1859) and with his own book **Practical Falconry** (1869), he did much to encourage beginners and create some understanding of falconry. As with so many other falconers he started as a boy with a kestrel. In 1851 he first met another falconer, William Brodrick. In that year he travelled to Northumberland and stayed at Belford for a fortnight, learning all that Brodrick could teach him of falcons and falconry. Brodrick gave Freeman a female merlin, **'Pearl'**. He returned home to Northampton and flew **'Pearl'** at larks and pigeons until 23 April, 1852, when he lost her, the fate of so many good hawks.

For many years Freeman flew merlins and sparrowhawks with great success both in Northampton and later in Cheshire, where he removed, living at Wild Boar Clough Parsonage. Some time after his first meeting

30

with Mr Brodrick he was again given a hawk, this time a peregrine tiercel from Lundy, the island in the Bristol Channel famous for its peregrines. Brodrick had moved from Northumberland to Devon and for several years was able to obtain eyass peregrines from Lundy for himself and his friends. The tiercel flew so well at hack that Freeman knew he had something special and, for fear of losing him, took him up after only a fortnight of freedom. Named 'Black Cloud' he became, in Freeman's own words, 'one of the best peregrines I ever had in my life'. This tiercel waited patiently on high and was very good at pigeons and partridges. He was killed while partridge hawking in Somerset by a man with a stick.

Being in suitable country and fortunate in his neighbours who freely gave permission for Freeman to fly his falcons on their grouse moors, he turned to grouse as the quarry, and from about 1855 enjoyed excellent sport with no need to go far from his home. Of his eyass peregrine falcons flown at grouse, the best remembered are 'Storm Cloud', a big gentle falcon who was equally as good at rooks and pigeons and would come to the hand like a goshawk, although always flown in high condition, and 'Princess', a small falcon who waited on high from the very beginning and was a grouse hawk of the very best. To quote Freeman: *To see this little falcon on the wing was a thing to be freshly remembered through life. From a high pitch she shot forward at the rising of a grouse at a rate which startled those who saw it. When at length I really lost her, I have no doubt she was shot. An excellent and noble friend of mine saw her last flight, and sent me two peregrines from Scotland as soon afterwards as he could. I have her photograph — a very good one; but that is all left me now of the 'Princess' — except, indeed, the memory of those bright days we have spent together on the hills, and the great wish that I could see her once more, even if it were only as she dashed across this valley, with a thing like a dark ball twenty yards before her, making my heart leap as she went.*

One further falcon, hacked for nearly six weeks and only taken up by chance, was a large powerful falcon named 'Islay' after her Scottish birthplace from where she was taken in 1865. Freeman claimed that as a hawk to kill game with, he would back her against any trained hawk in the world.

Church House, Shrewton. Headquarters of
the Old Hawking Club

3
The Old Hawking Club

In the year 1863 the Hon Cecil Duncombe and Major Charles Hawkins Fisher started spring rook hawking on Salisbury Plain. They made their headquarters at The Bustard Inn, beside the old direct road from Devizes to Salisbury. Robert Barr was employed as falconer and they had a first-rate team of six or seven red passage falcons, the first that had been imported for some years from Valkenswaard. The following year a small club was formed that blossomed into the Old Hawking Club. Robert Barr continued as Club falconer and the manager was that famous old falconer, once of the Loo Club, Edward Clough Newcome. To his home in Norfolk the hawks and falconer repaired each year after the campaign at rooks and still managed the occasional flight at a heron.

In its first year the Club membership stood at seven: the Hon Cecil Duncombe, Lord Lilford, the Maharajah Dhuleep Singh, Mr Amherst, Colonel Brooksbank, A. E. Knox and Edward Clough Newcome. In addition to the rook hawking, some good grouse hawking was enjoyed in Perthshire on a moor taken for that purpose by Maharajah Dhuleep Singh.

A club was started in 1866, in France, called the Champagne Hawking Club. John Barr, brother to Robert, was with them and for three seasons he showed excellent sport on the open country near Châlons. The quarry was rook, magpies, partridges, stone curlew and the little bustard, the last being particularly difficult. After 1869 the hawks continued under the management of Comte Alfonso de Aldama and in 1870 were sent to the home of Dhuleep Singh at Elveden Hall, Thetford, as war had broken out between Germany and France. In 1869 Dhuleep Singh sent John Barr and his nephew, Jamie, to Iceland to catch some gyrfalcons. So successful were they that they returned with thirty-three of these lovely falcons, using some half-a-dozen ponies to feed them on the voyage. These gyrs were all trained and some were entered to hares.

In the autumn of 1869 the Champagne Club hawks were taken to Grandtully Castle in Scotland, under the capable care of John Barr. There his brother Robert joined him with the hawks of the Marquess of Bute, and together the brothers, with a mixed team of both passage, haggard and eyass peregrines, produced the best of grouse hawking for their own and their employers' pleasure. Two hawks in particular flew with distinction, 'Granny', an old haggard, and 'Aurora', a very

The Hon Cecil Duncombe, brother of Ernest Feversham, member of the Old Hawking Club

The Hon Gerald Lascelles, Manager and Secretary to the Old Hawking Club from 1872 until 1914

tiny passage falcon, both the property of Comte Alfonso de Aldama.

In 1866 the 17-year-old Gerald Lascelles, son of the 4th Earl of Harewood, spent his Easter holidays rook hawking on Salisbury Plain with the members of the Old Hawking Club. There he met Edward Newcome for the first time. Two years later Gerald Lascelles went to Cambridge and from there often drove over to Feltwell for a day or two to see more hawking. In the spring of 1870 he and Newcome were invited to stay at Elveden Hall by Dhuleep Singh to see the gyrfalcons that John Barr had brought back from Iceland and to inspect the hawks of the Champagne Hawking Club. The Club hawks were mainly peregrines, of

Falconers' Horses

which there were about seventeen, and a few goshawks. The Maharajah, beside a great number of gyrfalcons, had a team of peregrines, a very fine saker and a few other hawks. Some of the gyrs were flown to the lure and three of them, in the opinion of Mr Newcome, were probably the finest performers that he had ever seen. Sadly, within a year nearly all of these lovely falcons were dead.

As a boy Lascelles had learnt much of hawking from Sir Charles Slingsby of Scriven. In his summer holidays Lascelles would ride over to Scriven, not thirteen miles from his family home at Harewood, and there with Sir Charles and a friend, Mr Bower, they would enjoy first-rate sport with a sparrowhawk at blackbirds and thrushes. Eventually came the day when he rode home to Harewood with sparrowhawk on fist. At Cambridge he was given a passage tiercel by Edward Newcome and kept a dog, organizing the necessary screen perch in his rooms at Magdalene.

On 22 September, 1871, Mr Newcome died in his sixty-second year. James Edmund Harting, writing of him said: *On field or fen, on moor or mere, by the riverside or on a racecourse, no man had more friends and fewer enemies than the late Edward Clough Newcome. But from his own Norfolk 'brecks' to the bogs of Ireland, from Salisbury Plain to the heaths of Brabant and the fells of Norway, he, from his boyhood, followed the sport of Falconry more keenly than any other; sharing its comparative prosperity of fifty years since; keeping alive its traditions when its practise had all but expired; reviving it with his own enthusiasm, by infecting others, had given promise of its continuance; and performing feats hitherto unknown in the annals of the art. Untiring in his devotion, even by the drudgery of the labour of love he undertook, as an efficient falconer he was unequalled by professionals or amateurs.*

35

A peregrine belonging to the Old Hawking Club

Prior to Mr Newcome's death the Hawking Club had closed down and Robert Barr went to work for the Marquess of Bute. The hawks were divided up amongst the members and Cecil Duncombe gave the falcon that came to him to Gerald Lascelles. In the spring of 1870 Lascelles, with two peregrines of his own, joined Robert Barr at Market Lavington on the edge of Salisbury Plain. On the way to Wiltshire from Harewood Lascelles stayed one day in London and, going to Tattersalls, bought a pony, it being essential for following a flight in rook hawking. The pony turned out to be a first-class hack and carried a hawk with no concern. Both Barr and Lascelles entered their hawks to rooks and had a certain amount of sport.

Towards the end of the following year Gerald Lascelles, Cecil Duncombe and Mr A. E. Knox met at Gordon Castle as guests of the Duke of Richmond. There they discussed the idea of starting up the Old Hawking Club again. Letters were sent to all the original members such as Lord Lilford and Colonel Brooksbank, and to others they thought might be interested. All the old members came forward with support for the idea, Lord Lilford very generously helping with the finance needed. Lascelles wrote to John Barr asking him to become the Club falconer, his brother Robert having died the previous year at Cardiff Castle. Gerald Lascelles was made manager and Hon Secretary of the Old Hawking Club, a post he held until the outbreak of the First World War in 1914. A start was made in the spring of 1872 with a particularly good team of passage falcons at rooks on the downland of Wiltshire and Berkshire, the Club hawks being kept at Oakhurst, part of the Harewood Estates, near Leeds, for the rest of the year. The following season John Frost, who had assisted Barr the previous year, became head falconer to the Club and held the post until his death in 1890.

For a while after leaving Cambridge Lascelles worked in the City at Lloyd's; then, in 1875, he married and removed to Leeds. There he studied land agency and in 1880 was appointed Deputy Surveyor of the New Forest and other Crown woodlands in Hampshire, totalling over 64,000 acres. He lived in the Queen's House, the old manor house of Lyndhurst, that in its earlier days had been retained for the use of Royal hunting parties. The hawks and falconer of the Old Hawking Club also moved to Lyndhurst, mews being set up in what had been the old stables, where many people contrived to get a look at them.

In the summer of each year young peregrines, usually eight or nine in number, would be flown at 'hack' at Lyndhurst. The young hawks, at perfect liberty, were sure to return for their food each evening until able to kill for themselves. They created great interest among locals and visitors alike and, once strong on the wing, they would attract an audience of perhaps fifty or more people who came in the evenings to watch the aerial acrobatics and excited flying of the growing eyasses. At liberty for three to five weeks, then taken up and trained, some of them would be flying again in a matter of a few weeks, perhaps killing their first grouse five hundred miles north of where they had learnt to use their wings.

In addition to the eyass peregrines, obtained from eyries as far afield as Donegal, the Isle of Wight and the Orkneys, each year the Club would

36

English and French falconers on Salisbury Plain for the spring rook hawking.
left to right: A. Pichot, J. E. Harting, George Oxer (Club Falconer), A. Belvalette, W. H. St Quintin, Hon Gerald Lascelles (Hon Sec. to the O.H.C.), 'Jack' Frost, Arthur Newall, E. Hare, W. M. Clarke, B. Heywood Jones.

purchase a number of freshly caught passage peregrines, usually six or eight, from the Dutch falconers at Valkenswaard. These, together with any ordered by individuals in England, would be collected by the Club falconer, who would travel over to Holland and stay there, training the fresh-taken hawks, until the orders were completed. These passage hawks were all initially entered to rook during the annual campaign on the Wiltshire Downs in March and April. Rook hawking being the major feature of the Club's activities, nearly all members gathered there to stay in one of the old inns, The George at Amesbury, The Crown Hotel, Everleigh, The Bustard Inn and others. Eventually Lascelles bought Church House in the village of Shrewton which became the headquarters of the Club for the rook hawking. Rooms were also found at various houses in the village to accommodate those of the members and guests who couldn't fit into Church House, but all would gather there after hawking.

At that time the Plain had not become a military training area, now all grass and scrub, but was open farmland with a good portion of arable land to attract the rooks searching for feeding in the spring. To obtain the best rook hawking it is necessary to have open country and only to fly at rooks well away from cover. In the spring of the year, when the hen birds

Feeding up a rook hawk

The Old Hawking Club on the Plain

Peregrines at Langwell, the highland home of the Duke of Portland, a member of the O.H.C.

are busy repairing the rookery and nesting, when the old male, or stag rooks, are feeding far away on the open downland, then rook hawking is at its finest. The very best flights were obtained at rooks on passage, flying out or returning from feeding. Flown directly into the wind, the falcon would attempt to get above the rook. The rook meanwhile, cut off from downwind escape by the approaching falcon, would attempt to stay above the hawk. So they would ring up and a classic flight, similar in many ways to the heron hawking of old, would be enjoyed. Soon, high overhead, they would drift in their circling, downwind, and then the falconers would ride hard to keep them in sight.

A good pony, quiet enough to allow the falconer to carry a hawk, was absolutely necessary. One mounted a hawking pony from the wrong side as the hawk was on the left fist. It also needed to be able to gallop on a bit and then to stand patiently while the falconer lifted the hawk from its kill or took it down to the lure. The Old Hawking Club also used a light game cart in which the hawks travelled on screen perches, well protected from the wild spring weather on Salisbury Plain.

Year by year the Club members enjoyed their sport, often joined by members of the French Hawking Club. Other members, perhaps more interested in game hawking, would make use of the Club servants and hawks. Such a one was the Duke of Portland who for some years had the hawks at Langwell in Caithness for grouse hawking. There John Frost, head falconer to the Club, died after serving the Club for eighteen seasons. Many guests were entertained by the Duke to a day on the hills with the hawks, although it would seem that the fashions of the day made walking hard for the ladies of the party. To quote from the Duke of Portland:

Soon after the hawks came to Langwell, the Duke and Duchess of Sutherland brought a party from Dunrobin, to pay me a visit and see the hawking. I met them at the Ord of Caithness, and showed them the sport between there and Langwell. The following letter from Lady Algernon Gordon-Lennox gives an amusing account of the visit:
My dear Portland,

I have a very vivid recollection of my first visit to Langwell when our party from Dunrobin invaded you: it consisted of the Duke and Duchess of Sutherland, General

39

and Mrs Marshall, Lord Suffield, Alex Leveson-Gower, and myself. You were an eligible bachelor, and I can hear 'Duchess Annie' impressing on Alex that she must wear her 'Sunday clothes' — a tartan skirt, velvet jacket, and a hat buried in long white ostrich feathers which meandered over her shoulders. Incidentally, I thought her much better dressed than I was! The Duchess's get up was even more impressive — brown velvet trimmed with innumerable rows of gold braid and high bronze kid boots! Hawking was the entertainment you provided for us, after an excellent luncheon, but the kid boots did not adapt themselves to walking through heather, and before many minutes, we watched with some amusement the Duke and Mrs Marshall ensconced on the skyline while the General and the Duchess found a lowlier point of vantage. As far as I remember, I think I carried on to the end, notwithstanding Lord Suffield's solicitude for my 'little feet' which made me wonder whether he thought I was suffering from corns!

Dandy and Berkeley Paget and Tom Boyce were staying with you, and of that little gathering only you and I are left to remember the sunshine, the purple of the heather, and how carefree we all were in those happy long-ago days!

Yours ever

Blanche Gordon-Lennox.

Lord Lilford, sadly too crippled to travel to the Plain for the rook hawking or north for the grouse, was still a great supporter of the Club and gave more than generously to maintain a sport he loved so well. Although his own country was not ideal for hawking, a steady reliable tiercel or falcon could usually be flown and he enjoyed some successful flights at partridge when, as often happened, the hawks were sent to spend a while with him.

His own mews were in the capable hands of Paul Mollen, brother to the famous Adrian. Mollen was also in charge of the many bird aviaries at Lord Lilford's home near Oundle in Northamptonshire.

Another member of the Old Hawking Club was the Duke of St Albans, Hereditary Grand Falconer of England. The post having at that time a stipend of some £1,200 per annum, he gave generously, with an agreement that should he be called upon to show falconry to the Royal

A kill; rook hawking with the O.H.C.

Family he should have the free use of the Club hawks and falconer. As for the sport itself, he did not care for it and never went out with the Club hawks. When the Duke commuted this income some years later, he withdrew from the Hawking Club.

In 1871 a Committee was made responsible for developing the four hundred acres of Alexandra Park as a public recreation ground. One of the many suggestions was that a mews should be set up there to revive the old sport of falconry. Accordingly in 1874 a club was started by Captain F. S. Dugmore, with Mr James Edmund Harting as secretary. It was known as the Falconry Club and had offices and mews at Alexandra Palace. A large number of hawks were kept on public view. It was planned that the Club should extend its activities to France, Ireland, Belgium, Holland and Spain, but although the Club hawks were flown in Ireland and exhibited in the Jardin d'Acclimatisation in Paris the whole idea was too large and unmanageable and after a few seasons the Club was broken up. John Barr had been employed as head falconer, with three or four assistants, and it was he who went to Norway to catch gyrfalcons in 1876. He succeeded in trapping ten gyrs, nine females and a jerkin, all birds of that year. Six were dead before the end of the year and of the four remaining, two were given to the Old Hawking Club, neither surviving long. Of the other two, one took rooks quite well on Epsom Downs. Besides the gyrs they had a number of peregrines which were flown at rooks, jackdaws, peewits and bagged gulls twice a week. The last mentioned were taken out in hampers and turned out on the downs. Apparently some gave splendid flights, being very shifty on the wing, and avoided the falcons' stoop with marvellous ease, some even managing to get away altogether.

41

Thomas Mann of Hyde Hall,
Sawbridgeworth with his falconer, Alfred
Frost, mounted on his hawking pony

4
T.J. Mann

Throughout the second half of the nineteenth century the Old Hawking Club continued to be the hub of the sport in England. The membership was not large and the annual rook hawking was very much a private affair for Club members and their guests. No casual traveller crossing the Plain would be welcome as a spectator; if indeed they stopped to watch the sport a green-coated servant of the Club would be sent over to move them on.

Until 1890 the Club falconer was John Frost and his skill and knowledge ensured sport of the highest quality. In the spring of 1886 a total of 243 rooks and crows were taken on the Plain; the following season 209 rooks. In 1890, the year of Frost's death in Caithness while grouse hawking, 257 rooks and crows were taken in 293 flights. These scores clearly illustrate the consistently good sport that Club members enjoyed.

Beside the Old Hawking Club there were many private hawking establishments that showed excellent sport season after season. One such was the mews of T. J. Mann of Hyde Hall, Sawbridgeworth, in Hertfordshire. Each spring would see him and his man, Alfred Frost, brother of John Frost of the Old Hawking Club, enjoying rook hawking, often with that famous artist, George Lodge, on the far from ideal country around Chrishall, Ickleton and Chesterford on the borders of Essex and Cambridgeshire. Autumn would find them flying peregrine tiercels at partridge on Docking Heath in Norfolk. They invariably also had a goshawk to fly at rabbits and hares. Sometimes they would train a merlin or two for flights at larks. This they did in 1886, which year should perhaps be remembered as the first season that Mann flew his famous goshawk 'Shadow of Death'. In her first season she took 104 rabbits besides many various. In 1887 Mann had four tiercels for his campaign at partridge, of which the most successful was a tiercel rather confusingly named 'Lundy', as he in fact came from the island of Skomer. By 1891, the year that the old goshawk 'Shadow of Death' died, T.J. Mann had started using passage tiercels for partridges and in that season had a first-class game tiercel in 'Vigilant', who for four seasons did good work in Norfolk.

Even with as skilful a falconer as Alfred Frost good hawks were often lost, a fate of many of the best trained hawks, and the rook season of 1893 started badly in this way. Alfred Frost kept a diary and from it we can see what happened.

Intermewed peregrine falcon

Hawk transport in which hawks could travel protected from the rain and wind. A stop while 'Jingle' has his feed bag.

11 March, 1893: *Began Rook Hawking with a Haggard Falcon, 'Blackcloud', 'Aphrodite' and 'Minor'. Our first flight was with 'Aphrodite' she going up, put one stoop in, then left her Rook, so I took her down at Mr G. Jonas's farm. The second slip was with 'Blackcloud' at Rooks on Mr Jonas's heath. The Falcon going above them grandly and then started stooping. After three or four stoops the Rook put in at the Ickleton Grange road, the Falcon going to ground for it. The Rook came through the hedge and away goes the Falcon again ringing after, it again fetching it into the road fence where we hunted it some time but not enough of us to keep the Rook moving. Eventually Hawk and Rook started ringing again, and the Rook put in this time at Mr G. Jonas's farm, so had to give it up after one of the finest flights ever seen in Cambs. In the afternoon we flew 'Blackcloud' again. Much to my regret the last she flew with us. I slipped her at Rooks on Mr Bowen's heath but other Rooks were in the valley nearer Elmdon. She took to flying them and not being able to keep her in view was lost and never heard a word about her being seen anywhere. 'Aphrodite' had another slip but would not stick to her Rook.*

As can be seen, Frost gave both Rook and Falcon capital letters, quite rightly so for a rook falconer.

Hawks, hawking ponies and falconers travelled up for their day's sport

44

from Sawbridgeworth on the train to Chesterford Station. From there they could ride out in search of rooks, going out two or three days a week.

The following spring Mann had three rook hawks, two passage falcons of his own and an intermewed falcon, 'Olinda', belonging to the Old Hawking Club. She didn't turn out well, only adding two rooks and a Norfolk plover to the score, but the two passage falcons, 'Stratagem' and 'Startaway', took twenty-nine rooks and a jackdaw and twenty-one rooks respectively. Alfred Frost seemed to enjoy his work and his reports of flights certainly give a feeling of the excitement of it all.

19 April. *Then came a grand flight with* 'Stratagem' *off Mr Jonas's heath. The Rook being a good one went away over the top of the hill, over Mr Bowen's covert, refusing to put in till it got to the boundary fence (Essex and Cambs.) where in the zig-zag fence it put in lots of times, I helping the Falcon, the latter having had the Rook on the ground twice besides losing its tail. The Rook then got to a small belt, the Falcon going through the hedge for it where she got hung for a short time. The Rook, taking the advantage of it, went away downwind high up towards Mr Rolfe's farm.* 'Stratagem' *then took to flying again, went away above her Rook and then put in three clinking stoops, killing it in the third, high up in the air. I may say it's one of the best flights ever seen. I should say the Falcon stooped quite 30 times before killing.*

24 April. *Had a slip off the little heath with* 'Stratagem' *at a single Rook, it coming back to the road and put in at a little tree by the drill shed. After being put out, it again took to the Ickleton Grange road, where after a hunt we killed it.*

Two days later 'Stratagem' caught a rook very cleverly. Slipped next to Redlands Farm, she went after her rook close to the ground, the rook meanwhile being high up in the air. When nearly at the hedge the falcon skilfully threw herself up into the wind and was at once on terms with her rook. Getting above it, she made a grand stoop and bound to high up in the air.

Partridge hawking was not perhaps pursued in the grand style, Mann and Frost only flying the tiercels once or twice a week. However, some fine game tiercels were trained and flown over the years and judging from Frost's diary they certainly had exciting moments.

14 September. *In the afternoon went up to the heath, had first flight with* 'Vigilant'. *Put him up close to the crossroads then flushed our birds. He stooped and took one directly, killing it close against us.* 'Stormcloud' *fared worse. He flew three birds off the heath, knocked one down by the bank. The next he lost in the white turnips, Master running across to look for it. The third he knocked down in the thistle and rough grass on the old plain. This too was lost so I fed him.*

Partridge were not plentiful. Sometimes Frost was unable to fly the hawks through lack of quarry.

17 October. *Flew* 'Stormcloud' *on the heath. Found nothing so had to take him down again. Put him up again. This time I saw but one Partridge, that escaping at the crossroads before he could get a stoop in, so had to lure him down. In the afternoon I flew him by East Wood, he waiting on grandly. We then flushed some Partridges and the Tiercel made a grand stoop and killed his bird. Put him up again over the swedes next Burnham road, he again waiting on high. A greenfinch got up, the Tiercel stooped and cut it down dead close to Mr Lodge and before Mr Lodge could get it the Tiercel had turned and taken it, carrying it to East Wood, then away over the top of the wood, I finding him, but not before he had eaten his little fry.*

The tiercels finished the season with forty-four partridge to their credit. Three fresh-taken passage peregrines arrived from Holland — 'Aurora' and 'Avalanche', falcons, and 'Acrobat', a tiercel.

The following rook season started on 23 March. 'Startaway' died on 15 March so the team consisted of the intermewed falcon, 'Stratagem', and 'Avalanche' and 'Aurora', the two first-season falcons, although the last falcon started the campaign with a bad attack of 'croaks'. 'Stratagem' killed on her first flight of the season but 'Avalanche' checked from her rook and, seeing a kestrel hovering in the air, she went and took it before the kestrel saw her. Flown again, she took her rook well and was fed up on it. Out again three days later, only 'Stratagem' was flown, it being wet. In a long flight she put a rook into farm premises where a boy threw a starling that he had shot out to her. On Frost galloping up, he saw the lad with the gun and got him to shoot the rook while he carefully picked up his falcon.

One of the golden rules of rook hawking is to make sure there are no rooks downwind of where a hawk is flown. How often do falconers regret that they did not observe this rule, the outcome being a lost hawk. So it happened with the falconers of other times and on 23 April Alfred Frost did just this. *Then back to Middle Farm and slipped* 'Stratagem' *at Rooks west side of the farm. Some now being downwind on the east side she took to flying them, not getting on terms with them till they reached Ickleton at the Abbey where they beat her — we then lost her for about two hours, I finding her then on a pigeon and had to wind her up as she took to carrying, Joe coming up and helped me.*

On another occasion 'Stratagem' was flown at a rook and killed a partridge. On the way back to the falconer, after putting rooks into a farm some way off, a brace of partridges got up. The falcon knocked one to the ground and then went down after it, scrambling about on the ground for some time before she caught it. The other partridge chased the falcon as they scrabbled on the ground and kept it up until the other was taken, and this Frost rescued and released to join its mate, quite unhurt.

'Stormcloud' and 'Acrobat', the two tiercels, both died in the summer of '95, but were replaced by three eyass tiercels from Major Radclyffe at Hyde in Dorset and another tiercel from Mr Stevens from Carmarthen

Young peregrine tiercel at hack

46

named 'Rambler'. The old tiercel 'Vigilant' made up the team, with a new female goshawk, 'Valkyrie'. Very few partridges were to be found and they had little sport.

Two new passage tiercels arrived in December from Mollen and they were named 'Rocket' and 'Rufus', but, losing both 'Stratagem' and 'Avalanche', they only had a single intermewed falcon for the rook hawking in 1896. They made a start on 20 March and killed a rook first flight.

Many mornings it was wet and on arriving at the station they had to shelter there for the rain to abate. But despite the weather they had a good season, on quite a few occasions 'Aurora' taking four rooks in the day. That autumn they had no hawking in Norfolk as Frost had no tiercels, the old hawks having died. At the end of September Major Fisher sent them a young tiercel and a falcon, deep in the moult. Frost finally had a few kills with the tiercel, which mounted and waited on in good style.

47

Hawks weathering on the lawn

In December, 1896, Mollen sent over four passage hawks: two falcons named 'Slaughter' and 'Soarer', and two tiercels 'Sportsman' and 'Speedy'. They began the season on 24 March, 1897 with two kills, one to 'Aurora', the old falcon, and one to 'Slaughter'. Again the season was one of storms and gale-force winds, the ground being so wet and slippery that on more than one occasion Frost notes that, in the gallop after a flight, both falconer and horse would end up rolling over and over in the mud. In such windy weather it was inevitable that hawks would be left out overnight on a kill. This happened on 21 April when, after a blank day, 'Aurora' went away down the wind. After an early morning train journey Frost luckily found her close to the railway station at Chesterford.

Despite the weather, some fine flying by the falcons made up for getting soaked to the skin. One such flight was on 1 May :

Had first flight off Mr Scale's hill by his off farm and after getting in three stoops the Rook took to ringing, the Falcon ditto, going away over the farm. Here I think the Falcon changed Rooks, she going away as if going to Mr Ickles's, where she put a Rook in there and hunted it in and out several times. They both then went in a tree in the bottom. I rode up, put out the Rook, the Falcon going away same time. Then some more ringing. Eventually the Rook tried hard to put in again, same place, the Falcon putting three grand stoops in and killed within five yards of the horse's nose.

On the last day of the season a flight to remember :

5 May. *After a time had another flight from the same place, (close to Mr Jonas's farm) the Rook getting to the farm where it put in, 'Slaughter' going to ground for it but, being put out, the Rook started ringing, the Falcon following suit (and, a N.W.*

48

wind blowing, the Rook could not get over the hill to the rookery). After getting up a tremendous height the Rook began shutting in, the Falcon getting stoop after stoop in before the Rook could put in again at the farm. This time 'Slaughter' tried to take it in the trees but putting the Rook out again both started ringing for fully five minutes. Then again the Rook tried for the farm and again put in, then again more ringing, only to come into the farm again. I then put the Rook out and the Falcon took (and well she deserved it) — the best flight of the season. In the afternoon I flew her again off Mr Nash's land, she taking her Rook first stoop.

So, season after season, both rook and partridge hawking, T. J. Mann and his falconer Frost had their sport, their exciting moments and their disappointments. Occasionally amusing incidents occurred as once when rook hawking early in the season. A hard-pressed rook, looking desperately for some cover in which to escape the stoops of a falcon, put in among some countrywomen picking and bagging up potatoes. Bravely the falcon stooped through the jumble of potato sacks and women, the rook immediately going to ground under the heavy long black skirts of a solidly built farm labourer's wife. Frost and the others galloped up on their ponies excitedly shouting at the ladies to serve the falcon who was patiently circling overhead. But by now the sympathies of the ladies were with the rook and they refused to move. Frost's immediate response was, 'Shall you push her over, Master, or shall I?' But manners overruled sporting instincts and, taking the falcon down to the lure, the hawking party moved well away from the potato field before recommencing their interrupted day.

49

5
W.H. St Quintin

When John Frost died his place was taken by George Oxer, who had trained under John Frost at Oakhurst and had spent some years with him as under-falconer before going as head falconer to Mr W. H. St Quintin of Scampston Hall. A long-time member of the Old Hawking Club, Herbert St Quintin not only regularly journeyed to Wiltshire to enjoy the spring rook hawking but also kept a team of hawks for game hawking and for flights at seagulls at which he was most successful.

Although not a strong man, Herbert St Quintin pursued his interests with great enthusiasm. At his lovely home on the Yorkshire Wolds he kept a huge collection of birds and wildfowl. Many were the successes he had at breeding rare and unusual species and this interest led to his lifelong friendship with Lord Lilford and Mr Meade-Waldo. Scampston Hall made the most perfect setting for an enthusiastic falconer, and in the country about, in Scotland and in Wiltshire, St Quintin saw and enjoyed the very best of sport.

First introduced to falconry by Gerald Lascelles at Oakhurst on the Harewood Estates, and by Cecil Duncombe, second son of Lord Feversham, who was later to become his father-in-law, Herbert St Quintin was soon a regular member of the small, select and happy group that met on the Plain each spring, then staying at The George Inn, Amesbury. Most of the day's sport was recorded by St Quintin in his neat handwriting and is of interest to those of us who have tried to catch spring rooks on the Plain in these difficult days. Certainly rooks were plentiful, wire fences unknown, and trees few and far between. But there were hazards, the very many sheep folds on the downs affording good cover to a hunted rook, and then, as now, all too often the rooks were in near the farms and villages.

Magpies appear to have been well scattered, and the excitement of magpie hawking was added to the thrills of rook hawking. On 22 April, 1879 Herbert St Quintin noted: *Captain Salvin joined the Club, bringing with him his well-known stud of kites and kestrels including the famous lanner, 'White-headed Bob'. [That day] 'Amazon' flew three flights well, and killed each time. 'Bois le Duc' twice, killed once: flew a long hard flight second time and was beat into a barn. 'Hollandaise' killed well after a hustle. 'Shooting Star' flew a tremendous fine ringing flight, but was beat in a fold at last. Second time killed first stoop. 'Wheel of Fortune' had a hard ringing flight then killed an easy one close to her. 'Princess'*

(opposite) W. H. St Quintin

A young goshawk on the screen perch

Ten peregrine falcons at the Old Hawking Club, Shrewton

flew well twice, and killed once, two good flights. Had a good flight at a magpie and killed. 'Northern Light' flew well. Eleven flights, eight rooks, one magpie.

23 April. *Towards Idmiston. G. Lascelles went away early. A quiet day's sport. 'Princess' killed easily. Second time put in and had a rat hunt in gorse and caught hold. Let go on reaching the ground, and the rook got away, then had some magnificent ringing, much higher than any this year, put in a terrific stoop, into gorse again, and killed after a rat hunt. 'Amazon' killed three times, last time a very long slip. She never saw them and wheeled round, when the rooks had nearly a quarter of a mile start; she then tried hard and flew her best, got above and killed fourth stoop, high in the air. 'Bois le Duc' flew well and killed twice with first stoops, long slips. 'Hollandaise' flew well and killed after putting into some premises. 'Shooting Star' flew hard and put in, after a rat hunt she raked away and killed. Eleven flights (including one of the nestling falcons, 'Northern Light', at some rooks overhead which she never saw) and ten kills. Then had a good flight at a magpie and 'Northern Light' killed after a good flight on top of Beacon Hill.*

24 April. *Bulford, Figheldean, etc. 'Amazon' killed after a rat hunt, 'Bois le Duc' the same. 'Princess' killed in rare form, second time got beaten to rookery after putting in two different folds. 'Hollandaise' and 'Shooting Star' each got beat after rat hunts, and 'Wheel of Fortune' got beaten into some osiers and sat down. Hustled a magpie with 'Northern Light' and 'Dauntless' (tiercel) and the latter killed. Seven flights, three rooks and one magpie. Brooksbank came.*

These notes give a fair idea of the ups and downs of the sport.

In the autumn of 1879 St Quintin flew his hawks at partridges near his home and then travelled to Ireland to try his tiercels at magpies. He took with him four tiercels, 'Meteor', 'Buccaneer', 'Prefect' and 'Prince Imperial', and two falcons, 'Galatea' and 'Northern Light'. The hawks were flown on the Curragh in Kildare and at Fermoy in Co Cork between 22 October and 6 November inclusive, and in this short season took forty-nine magpies, ten rooks and a peewit. Of this total twenty-six magpies were taken by one of the tiercels, 'Buccaneer'. Sadly, on the last

day of the Irish tour a cat attacked 'Buccaneer' and 'Galatea' at their blocks and both hawks died within the week of blood poisoning. On returning to Yorkshire the tiercels quickly returned to their usual quarry, flying the rest of the season at partridges.

St Quintin spent March, April and May of 1880 at The Crown Inn, Everleigh. At the start he was much on his own, most members being occupied with the Elections. Frost was very backward with getting the hawks ready. The stud consisted of 'Princess', now two years old, and 'Bois le Duc', a fourth-season falcon, and nine young passage falcons, besides a promising tiercel of Brooksbank's, a high flyer though never hacked. This tiercel was later lost while being exercised to the lure.

'Princess' soon got into her stride and killed the most rooks at the beginning of the season but was unfortunately lost near Amesbury through people giving false information as to a kill. She hung about for some time and killed a mallard in the water meadows near Amesbury church but was not recovered. Earlier in the season she had started taking jackdaws and spent a night out through this.

The Club hawk van on the Plain

John Frost, Head falconer to the Old
Hawking Club

'Bois le Duc' started the season well but became very shifty and had to
be snared several times. This made her very wild and unsteady and they
dared not fly her. The most promising of the young falcons was
'Makeshift', a very fair but not brilliant hawk. She was kept for the
following season, they attempting to fly her right through the summer to
get her as clever as possible, and then put her down to moult.

'Cockatrice', a fine flyer but not good at rooks, went to Herbert St
Quintin, 'Agrael' went to Colonel Brooksbank. This falcon was remarkably
tame and easy to handle and made a useful gamehawk on the Wolds.
'Satanella', a very fine and tiny falcon, was kept by the Club as a possible
game hawk; 'Candace', a large dark falcon, one of the two finest that
Adrian Mollen ever saw, was also kept by the Club. This falcon, with
great powers of flight, would not take to rooks for a very long time, but
well repaid the time given to her and was one of the stars of the team of
rook hawks the following season.

As are most falconers, St Quintin was keen on all bird life and in his notes on the season of 1880 he recorded the following:

Hobbies. *Saw hobbies several times about a wood between Druid's Head and Stonehenge. The pair showed their marvellous powers of flight to perfection one day in pursuit of our tiercels who had followed a magpie for a long distance into their wood (Scots firs). They are easily distinguishable by their sharp swift-like wings.*

Peregrines. *Saw at Everleigh at different times: an old tiercel, ditto with very ragged wings, a young falcon, and, at Amesbury, or rather in the 'Bustard' country, another tiercel. It is said that there is again a pair of peregrines about Salisbury Cathedral spire. They were said to have bred there last year and a boy to have taken the eggs. Unfortunately none of our members have been over to see them.*

Buzzard. *I saw one while staying at Everleigh and some of the others saw one from Amesbury.*

Harrier. *One was seen by some of our fellows from Amesbury. Species uncertain.*

Merlin. *Many seen. One day one came right up to G. Oxer's lure, within a few yards of him and Frost.*

Dotterel. *Saw a pair one day in the 'Bustard' country, exceedingly tame, rode within ten yards of them and then they only ran. There were men and horses cleaning and burning 'wicks' all round them. Tried to get the tiercels to fly them but the dotterel went off hard, before they got to their pitch.*

Thick-knee Plover. *Saw many of them and had three flights at them (one ending we thought in a rabbit hole) but we had no hawk used to take them and we feared to spoil the best rook hawks by taking them from their proper quarry.*

The following season started on 17 March when 'Amesbury', a falcon caught on the Plain, and the only falcon ready to try, took her first rook well at a sheep fold. St Quintin's little tiercel 'Aide de Camp' flew well at a magpie and killed. The weather that spring was very stormy which made it impossible to hawk on many of the days. Nevertheless the score for the season was 167 head and many of the flights were of the highest class. After some days of storms the hawks were taken out on the 22nd towards Ludgershall. 'Amesbury' flew a most excellent flight, going up to her rook despite the high wind, climbing to a great height. She cut out the rook's tail with her first stoop but did not hold it. The falcon then mounted very high, taking her time and not stooping until the rook was just in the right place. She then put in a tremendous stoop and bound to the rook high up in the air over Hougoumont Farm.

By 26 March most of the hawks were flying, but the little falcon 'Amesbury' was really into her stride and on the Ludgershall road she had a really grand flight. The rooks had got very high in the air before the falcon got to them but she fetched them down to some haystacks. She chivvied them about and her rook soon left and a wonderful ringing flight followed, the rook trying hard for the Everleigh rookery. Finally the little falcon got high over her rook and drove him down with a fine stoop, followed quickly by another, in which she hit the rook hard, then ran into him and bound to. As St Quintin noted: *This is, I think, the finest flight I ever saw for high ringing and fine quick stoops: distance about half a mile.*

On the 28th Club members went out with the Tedworth Hounds in the morning, crossing the downs in the afternoon to Beach's Barn, near Saddler's Pit, where the falconers awaited them with the hawks. 'Amesbury' flew an easy one and killed first stoop. Then 'Candace', the

blue falcon, and 'Morgiana' were flown together. The old hawk did all the work, fetching the rook down, but the young falcon then joined in and they stooped alternately until the young falcon killed. 'Candace' was then flown again with another of the young hawks. The old falcon flew in splendid form; going up to her rook with great pace, and, stooping splendidly, she killed, the young falcon going after other rooks with little success. On the last day of March 'Gitana', the most promising of the young entry, was lost. At 7.30 the next morning Frost found the falcon at Bulford with a full crop. He followed her all day and finally snared her at Bulford rookery at 5.45 pm. He saw several wild peregrines that day.

Five days later 'Creole', St Quintin's Indian falcon, was lost but brought home in the morning in a flour sack. A miller from the village of Milston caught her on a pigeon. This falcon was the cause of much correspondence as to her species and on 4 April Herbert St Quintin received a letter from Francis Salvin who seemed quite confident of solving the mystery:

Whitmoor House
Guildford.

Dear St Quintin,

Thanks for your interesting letter. I think I can tell you what your foreign hawk is when I see it which I hope will be just after Easter. I wonder what's to do with the falcon's foot. If from the trap I think glycerine with chloride of zinc would cure it. That

(opposite) A female goshawk in 'yarak'

A cadge of peregrines ready for the moor

must have been a grand flight at the old carrion crow! With varvels you can slip **at once** *so she would have recaught the rascal. I never have seen varvels catch on twigs but* **I have seen** *jesses with slits catch and hang a hawk up.*

We have had nearly a week of very high wind and with you it must have been a caution. I fly 'Spiteful' *(goshawk) about the house in all this wind for she likes it, and it's grand to see her and I can trust her.*

A friend, Mr Angelo [well known for his deer hounds wit which he coursed red deer in Scotland], his niece, Miss Angelo and a Miss Elmhirst, a splendid rider, want very much to bring horses to Amesbury to see some more hawking for I have 'blooded them' at Brighton and so whet their appetites. Our side of the Inn will be full I suppose but if the other side won't hold them could you inquire if they could take a lodging for a week?

Yours sincerely,
F. H. Salvin

P.S. You call your foreign hawk 'a Lanner or what not'; if from India it cannot be a Lanner, they don't exist there.

'Creole' turned out to be a small passage falcon.

A further letter from Salvin later that year is also of interest.

Whitmoor House
Guildford.
21 November, 1881.

My dear St Quintin,

Many thanks for your letter. It is just the report I so much wanted and which I could not get out of the Brooksbanks who (dad and son) are bad at letters.

Brodrick is about giving a lecture on 'Hawks and Hawking' to a Naturalists' Club and wants all information as to what hawks have killed. I suppose 'Parachute' *is a* **great and steady mounter** *is she not? My mature Gos,* 'The Garroter' *is perfect. She did not fly the first year that she was taken from the nest, but she had been manned when I got her last spring. Ai moulted her at* **the block** *and will now back her against a gunner at gun range within which space she never misses. She killed ten rabbits one evening. I left her in Scotland and the last report was that she had taken sixty-eight rabbits and a hare, nine and a half pounds! She was to be taken against* **The Hill Tribes** *(the mountain or blue hares) after which I was to have another report which is looked for daily. These hares are very small as you know. If she trees which is very seldom, she comes down on the lure at once . . .*

Of course one cannot compare a Gos with the grand flight of the falcons but the Gos is very good fun for a bye day. Mine kept a shooting box in rabbits and the cormorants in white trout.[1] There is a curious trait in the character of mine: when she kills I cannot lose her tho' it may be in thick cover for she makes an awful noise for me to come up and put a stiletto into the quarry.

I long to hear what you do with the Lanner[2] when ready. The Club hawks and Frost have arrived.

Yours sincerely,
F. H. Salvin

In 1882 St. Quintin took Achinduich Moor in Sutherland for grouse hawking and shooting. Salvin had advised him as to what type of ground was suited to the sport: *I hope you may get a suitable moor. What you want for grouse hawking is a* **flat** *basin with* **hills** *all round. A falcon cannot be lost in such a moor and I have seen several. What makes the flight rather a risky one is the bad colour of the ground for marking and the length of the flight.*

---

[1]This was in Skye where Salvin's trained cormorants took many sea-trout.
[2]A wild-caught Lanner St Quintin obtained from Africa.

58

Feeding up a rook hawk

St Quintin and Colonel Brooksbank, with a mixed team of Club hawks, together with some of their own, with John Frost, the Club falconer, and George Oxer, St Quintin's personal falconer, achieved the outstanding score of 100 brace of grouse between 12 August and 14 September. This score was the more remarkable in that the hawks were only flown in the afternoons, weather permitting.

Hawks:	Grouse	Partridge	Pheasant	Hares	Sundries	TOTAL
'Parachute' eyass falcon 2 years	57	76	5	3	5	146
'Vesta' eyass falcon 1 year	43	18	—	—	1	62
'Virginia' eyass falcon 1 year	3	1	—	—	—	4
'Angela' passage falcon 2 years	36	—	—	—	—	36
'Creole' passage falcon 2 years	10	—	—	—	—	10
'Amesbury' passage falcon 3 years	32	—	—	—	—	32
'Aide de Camp' eyass tiercel 1 year	16	9	—	—	1	26
'Belfry' eyass tiercel 1 year	3	—	—	—	—	3
	200	104	5	3	7	319

Achinduich was rented by Herbert St Quintin and Arthur Brooksbank for several seasons, although they never again reached the score of 1882. They usually shot for a few hours in the mornings and the hawks and falconers came out with the luncheon pony. They had a useful team of lemon and white setters, used for both the shooting and the hawking.

After the grouse hawking St Quintin would return to Scampston Hall, and from there would fly the hawks at partridges. They often carried a goshawk, hooded on the cadge, for flights at the odd rabbit. Each season a new hawk or two would be added to the team to replace those discarded or lost. Eyasses were taken and hacked and John Frost on his annual pilgrimage to Holland would bring back six or eight passage hawks for the Club and any hawks ordered from Holland by other Englishmen. Frost wrote to St Quintin on 14 November, 1883:

Valkenswaard
North Brabant
Holland.

Sir,

We have now twelve falcons, seven tiercels, six merlins and one goshawk, and still want one falcon to complete our number. Am getting on with the taming fairly well, one or two falcons are rather troublesome. I intend bringing the last-caught tiercels for you and have taken the first one in hand this evening. The tiercels I have selected for you are all neat made, smart birds, but not large, there is not a big tiercel among the lot. The falcons are a medium-sized lot, nothing grand about any of them.

I purpose returning to Lyndhurst the fore part of next week.

Your Obedient Servant
John Frost

John Frost, professional falconer, all-round sportsman, and close friend to many of the Old Hawking Club members, died in September, 1890 when only thirty-six years old. As Herbert St Quintin wrote: *This year was a very sad one for us, for in September our excellent Club Falconer, John*

Adrian Mollen and George Oxer with two fresh-caught peregrines at the Valkenswaard in Holland.

Frost, died at Langwell. He had not been really well since he had a double attack of influenza in the spring. Nevertheless he had had some excellent sport with the grouse hawks in Caithness, and none of us knew that there was any cause for anxiety about him — as a result Geo. Oxer left me to take Frost's place and Charles Frost, John's eldest son, came to me at Scampston. Paul Mollen, from Lilford, went over to Holland to bring back the passage hawks caught this autumn.

Frost's death also prompted this letter from Meade-Waldo:

8 October 1890

My dear Herbert,

I have not written to you since I heard of poor John Frost's death. I am so awfully sorry, he must have written that last letter to you quite a short while before he died. I thought he seemed so well and cheery in it. How will his place be filled? And what are the hawks doing? Jerry Lascelles has gone away north, he seems very cut up about it . .

I shall be very interested to hear what is done about a falconer in poor Jack's place, it is a very difficult if not almost impossible place to fill. I am so glad that 'Kismet' promises so well. I expect you are at the gulls now. What is 'Juno' doing? And 'Kaiser'?

Well, 'Kaiser' was doing well and on the day the letter was written he took a partridge in great style. 'Juno' was not so lucky, but made up for it by killing a pheasant on the following day.

Through the early '90's fine sport was enjoyed at game with 'Marmion', 'Maxim' and 'Lighting', the last also flown at gulls with 'Kismet', 'Lina', and 'Nemesis'. Much of the time master and falconers were out together but when St Quintin was away on business, then the falconers would go out on their own. So often on such occasions the sport is of the very best, but just now and again something goes wrong, perhaps a hawk is lost and the falconer must report this to his master.

'Osman', a peregrine tiercel, the property of Herbert St Quintin

The Lodge
Lowsthorpe.
22 October, 1893.

Sir,

I am sorry to say I have lost old 'Kismet'; we were flying at gulls on Thursday near the Gatehouse. They both flew the gull very hard across the stream, out of our sight. The falcon came back very soon after but I have not seen the tiercel since. Craske drove me a good way round yesterday and I made all inquiries I could but only heard of him once and that was about a hour after I lost him at Harp Lane. It has taken a lot of good time looking for him but I have got out with the game hawks in the afternoons. 'Norma' is doing well. She killed a good old cock pheasant one day last week and some very good hens. The tiercels killed a young cock on Thursday and on Friday 'Maxim' killed a hen himself. The goshawk of Sir Henry's [Boynton] is coming to hand now; he was over to look at her yesterday and wishes me to keep her till Thursday.

I Remain Sir
Your Obedient Servant
Charles Frost.

Now that George Oxer was Club falconer it became his duty to travel to Holland each year to collect the passage hawks ordered of Mollen. Adrian Mollen would then send out his accounts to his customers.

Valkenswaard
Holland
15 November, 1894

Sir,

I have heard from Mr G. Oxer that he arrived safe with the hawks at Lyndhurst, so I suppose you will have the two tiercels under your hands. It was an early passage this autumn; so I hope you will have the tiercels ready in good time for the seagulls, and hope you will have good sport as ever. I will also take the liberty to enclose my account for the hawks I caught for you this passage.

With best wishes,
I remain kindly
Yours Truly
A. Mollen

Note to W. H. St Quintin Esq.

For the Catch of 2 Tiercels	£6 -. -.
For taming	5. -.
2 hoods at the hawks	4. -.
Part of Box Cadge	2. -.
Total	£6.11. 0.

Gull hawking has the advantage over rook hawking that seagulls rarely, if ever, put into cover, other than water. Because of this Herbert St Quintin was able to fly gulls close to his home, in country far too wooded for the traditional rook hawking. One problem with entering to seagulls was the dislike most hawks had for gull flesh and occasionally St Quintin had to resort to the use of washed meat to make the hawks keen for blood. 'Destiny' sometimes required washed meat, but 'Impulse' certainly never needed it. In the enclosed country around Scampston a horse was not of much use and they usually managed to follow the flights on their feet. The length of flight was entirely dependent on the amount of wind. If the day was comparatively calm, one could almost walk after the flight, as, after the hawk had run up to the quarry, though the stoops were many and the ringing hard work, the birds would not get over very much ground in any particular direction. If the wind was fresh, the flight would generally be over in half a mile or less, though every now and again a flight might go a considerable distance.

The moult was, of course, a great difficulty when flying passage hawks in the autumn and winter. In St Quintin's opinion there was no great risk in flying them through the moult, although sometimes they would throw so many primaries at once that they might perhaps be laid off for three weeks to a month in the middle of the season.

Hard work at the lure was most essential to get hawks ready to fly at gulls. At Scampston they were busy with eyasses at game until the beginning of October, when they would get to work at the gull hawks. They would be called off to the lure in all weathers, the rougher the better, sometimes twice a day, and were not given a gull until they were in really hard condition. As St Quintin said, 'If hawks are short of work, and not in good wind, they cannot compete successfully with such a quarry as the seagull, with its untiring, buoyant flight.'

The winter of 1895/96 produced some good gull hawking. They started the season with an old falcon, 'Nerissa', and 'Owen', a tiercel.

17 December. *Flew the two hawks at herring gulls on the hillside opposite Rookdale Farm. Both went hard and drove one down the valley towards Shardale, the falcon coursing, and 'Owen' stooping well. At last the tiercel caught hold, and 'Nerissa', coming with a drive, knocked him off. On reaching the place we took 'Owen' down, but could not see the falcon. We had noticed the gull making off down the valley and at last concluded that 'Nerissa' had followed him, though the haze was so bad that we had not seen her. Spent the rest of the morning searching downwind, but saw nothing. Passing through Winteringham, heard that Mitchell, Cholmeley's keeper, had got the hawk, and found her at his house in a basket. She had killed the gull in the South Park, quite a mile and a half from where we had missed her. Unluckily she brought the gull down close to the keeper, who was rabbiting, and she was picked up at once, without being blooded. Went home very hopeful, after this proof of determination on the part of the old hawk.*

30 December. *Very foggy, but as I was anxious to show G.L. [Lascelles] a flight, we started out with the hawks. So thick that we could not use the glass, and we drove about a long time without seeing gulls. As a last chance we tried the South Park at Newton. There we found a small lot of herring gulls, but they were very restless and it was with some difficulty that we got a very poor slip; the light too being so bad that I feared the hawks would never get sighted. However, all went right, and the hawks rattled away downhill, amongst the trees and towards the house. The old falcon was first up and fetched one of the gulls with a fair stoop. However, she threw herself too wide, which is a fault of hers, and it looked as if she would hardly get on terms again with the gull, which had shifted from her stoop and was already well above her. We had quite lost sight of the tiercel in the fog and were glad indeed to see him come down with a real good stoop, from a fine height, right upon the gull's back, which fell to the ground and was quickly pinned by the falcon. A risky flight, but we came out of it alright, thanks to good luck!*

11 January. *Out Thirkleby way, hoping to see something of the falcon. Lots of*

*gulls. Flew 'Owen' twice in the morning, but he checked each time at rooks, and did
no good. On my way home saw a flock of gulls at some ploughs, in a nice place and
decided to give the tiercel another chance. He went hard and high; driving the gulls below
him down the valley, and then back to us. Finally getting one in the right place, he stooped
and killed a young herring gull, falling on the road, almost into my dog-cart.*

25 February. *High wind. Found a flock of common and herring gulls beyond
Rookdale. Very unsettled, but followed them up and at last found them sitting on a
fallow below Thirkleby. Wind very bad: 'Rocket' went up splendidly and fetched a
gull with a fine stoop, 'Owen' followed but struck the ground and disabled himself for
a time. 'Rocket', still flying hard, put in a cracker, and broke the gull's wing, and he
fell at our feet, 'Owen' so put off by his mishap that he would not even come into the
kill. Tried 'Nerissa' at rooks on our way home, near Shardale. She went over the rook
at which I slipped her, and which she might have killed, rattled off after a flock further
upwind, and did no good. Then turning downwind she raked off and it looked
dangerous, but she turned for a moment and we got her. Started her off to Lyndhurst
this evening.*

St Quintin's diaries continue the following season:

George Oxer on the lawn at Church House,
Shrewton

65

left to right: Captain Radclyffe, George Oxer and George Lascelles

17 October, 1896. *The first nice hawking day we have had for weeks. Gerald Lascelles out. George Oxer also out, who had brought with him my old falcon, 'Patience', and a beautiful little tiercel called 'Siegfried'. On our way to the Harpham Fields I flew 'Osman' over some rape, where I had marked some birds. He killed cleverly, trussing his bird as it skyed up to cross the beck. Having marked a covey in turnips, we hooded off 'Patience', but she sat in a tree. To tempt her out we flew 'Sorceress' (an eyass falcon), who got up nicely. Out came the old falcon and joined her at a very fair pitch. When the birds rose, the old one stooped at once and caught over the next fence. The young one, as usual, at first was rather slow in making up her mind but when she saw the covey crossing the next field, went hard and killed two, a pretty right and left! As there were still some birds left in the turnips, Gerald flew his tiercel, who killed very cleverly, though it was a bird that rose awkwardly before he had reached his pitch. 'Osman's' turn came next, but he played the fool and I do not think did quite his best when the covey was flushed, for they turned upwind and beat him. The tiercel soared and we lost sight of him in the direction of Thompson's Bridge. Moody went after him but we left the hawk out. After rather a long search, we marked a covey in a good place and flew 'Patience', who killed well. She killed again late, and was fed up. 'Siegfried' was tempted off by pigeons at the critical moment. When the birds rose, however, he gave us a sample of his style of mounting and stooping, and* *he, though so small a hawk, certainly is as good as any one we have had here for years past. In his next flight he killed in his best form — 4 brace. In the morning we had given the gull tiercels a capital chance at a common gull in Burton Field. But 'Saracen' did not go and after 'Rocket' had put in about three fine stoops he gave up. Gave them an easy one which 'Rocket' cracked over with a broken wing, first stoop. The eyass again declined to go.*

Sunday, 18 October. *Recovered 'Osman' at midday.*

31 October. *Began the day well by a pretty little flight at a common gull in Burton Fields. Both tiercels went very keen, at first dividing, the eyass fetching a common gull, while the passage hawk put in three or four stoops at a blackhead. Fortunately 'Rocket' came in to join 'Saracen', and we had some pretty stooping, the little hawks giving the quarry no rest and at last 'Rocket' caught hold, after perhaps six or eight stoops from each hawk. Great rejoicings, as the tiercels went well and the young one showing that he can put in some good work.*

As can be seen from the above, not every flight was a classic; but the results illustrate well the enthusiasm with which skilled gentlemen falconers such as Herbert St Quintin pursued the sport and maintained its standards of excellence.

6
Major Charles Hawkins Fisher

Sometimes it is by chance rather than design that one pursues a particular sport or hobby. So it was with Major Charles Hawkins Fisher of The Castle, Stroud, Gloucestershire.

In 1858 Major Fisher missed a train from Thetford station in Norfolk, and, having two hours to wait until the next train, he went for a stroll. Being in need of refreshment he made his way to a little inn, and there saw, for the first time in his life, a cadge of trained peregrines, attended by a cadge man. On inquiring about the hawks he was told they were the property of Mr Pells, so he entered the sanded parlour and made himself known to Mr John Pells, deputy falconer to the Duke of St Albans, Grand Falconer of England.

Pells then lived at Feltwell, and Fisher, keenly interested in all that he saw, telegraphed home that he was not to be expected. Soon Pells, cadgeman, hawks and Major Fisher were on their way in the pony cart to the falconer's home. So opened a new chapter in Major Fisher's life. By the merest chance he embraced the sport which then occupied his attention until his death at the age of seventy-six in 1901.

Charles Hawkins Fisher was the third son of Mr Paul Fisher, the well known historian of Stroud, who lived and continued working until the great age of ninety-four years. Charles was sent to Rugby, under Dr Arnold, where he was a contemporary of Tom Hughes. He continued his education at Brasenose College, Oxford and from there joined the 14th Light Dragoons. In 1854 he left the Regiment to join the Royal North Gloucester Militia, partly because it kept him at home and enabled him to enjoy the rural life of his own county, and partly because Colonel Kingscote, who then commanded the Regiment, was a personal friend and near neighbour. As quite a young man he had a severe fall out hunting which made it difficult for him to follow that sport as keenly as he wished. He therefore turned his attention to archery and shooting and later to falconry.

As an archer he won the Championship of England five times, in 1871, 1872, 1873, 1874 and 1887. Undoubtedly he was the most remarkable figure in English archery since the great Horace Ford. In perfection of style Fisher had no rival; his spare, wiry figure gave him a considerable natural advantage, of which he made the most. Certainly few archers delivered their arrows with a flight so beautiful as that achieved by Major

(opposite) Major Charles Hawkins Fisher, Riddlehamhope 1897

Major Fisher and Charles Radclyffe, Riddlehamhope 1897

left to right: William Rutford, assistant falconer, with 'Princess', Major Fisher with 'Lady Jane Grey' and James Rutford, falconer, with 'Lundy'

Fisher. But even archers have their off days, as Francis Kilvert noted in his Diary.

Friday 27 August, 1875. *Crossing the river at Normanton Hatches we walked along the hillside through meadows and barley fields till we came to the hospitable Manor House of Great Durnford, the seat of Mr John Pinckney, where we found Mr and Mrs Pinckney, Mr Charles Everett and Major Fisher, the Champion Archer of England, at luncheon . . . Major Fisher was not shooting like the Champion Archer of England and kept on dropping his arrows into the green. He was angry with the woodpigeons, because they divert his falcons from their game when he is hawking. 'A hunted pigeon', said the Major, 'is the fastest bird out. He will go considerably more than a mile a minute and away goes the falcon after him for miles.' He said also, 'A falcon is a true gentleman (Falcon gentle).' Major Fisher now keeps nothing but peregrines. He says the gyr-falcons are becoming very scarce. He asked Morris and myself to come to his hawking lodge at Chitterne, near Heytesbury, and see him hawk for rooks.*

Major Fisher's first hawk was a tiercel, 'Black Prince', which he bought from John Pells in 1858, and for some time after that date Pells continued to hack eyasses for Fisher, among them 'The Cardinal', an eyass tiercel from a Dorset eyrie who became a good rook hawk, and Major Fisher's first Lundy peregrines.

It wasn't long before Major Fisher was attracted by the idea of grouse hawking and in 1866 he joined Colonel Jones in taking Drumnasallie, a moor near Fassiefern in Argyllshire. Jamie Barr was with him as falconer and there they enjoyed shooting and hawking at grouse, both black and red, wild duck and woodcock. There Fisher witnessed a fine flight which is best described in his own words:

I made a line to beat out a wide bank of bracken, then brown with early autumn, and saw a bird, which I believed then to be a woodcock and the keeper a winged grouse, jump up in front. Had I but the courage of my convictions, and put my favourite falcon, called 'Taillie,' from her broken tail — Welsh hawk she, from the Glamorgan precipices of the Worms' Head — aloft, then she would probably have been saved much trouble, and we should have lost a glorious sight, and flight, for the day was stilly, bright, and lovely, and the sea-loch and its waves sparkled in the sun. No, I took her on my fist, and struck the hood in readiness, half disposed to believe in McPhee the gamekeeper. Just where I saw the bird spring, suddenly up went a fine woodcock. No winged bird she, but in full possession of the excellent pair that had not

left to right: Mrs George Simonds, George Simonds, Arthur Newall, Mrs Arthur Newall, Major Fisher and James Rutford

long before brought her (I suppose, for we do not know) from Finland, or elsewhere in the north of Argyll. I unhooded and cast 'Taillie' after her, and the flight began. This woodcock would have astonished sportsmen only used to their actions in a thick covert. Up and up she went in long zigzags, with precisely the style and action of her small relative, the common snipe, but mute. The falcon mounted rapidly in her train, though at a considerable disadvantage at first. I saw it was going to be a long affair, got out my glasses, and lay down on the heather, and on one side was my then falconer, Jamie Barr, one of the well-known family of Scotch falconers. There were once a father and three sons of that name (all falconers by profession), with most acute and trained vision, and on the other side the proud possessor of the best pair of eyes in all Argyll, if not in the West of Scotland — the so-called 'fox-hunter's' son, my gillie, Sandy Kennedy. This man got much employment in seeking sheep lost on the hills and mountains, and long practice had rendered his ancestral eyesight (his father's had been as good) equal to most glasses on the moor. The woodcock, with the falcon below and behind her, did not dare to come down or return – vestigia nulla retrorsum was her motto – and soon the pair of dots were high over the sea-loch, there a mile wide, the cock's point being evidently Morven, on the other side of the strait. Soon I called out, 'I can see but one'. Presently from Barr came, 'I canna see them'; from Kennedy, 'I ken 'em fine!' I hardly believed he could, for my own eyes were then far above average, and, aided by the best of Voigtlander's field-glasses, it was as much as I could do. Presently methought that the single dot in the sky which I still discerned became, instead of fainter, faintly more visible. 'They are coming back,' quoth Kennedy, and before long the spot had visibly increased, and the falconer Barr declared that he saw them once more. So did I, and so did all before long; for the woodcock, finding herself over the water, and unable to shake off her pursuer or gain the distant haven of Morven, had no alternative but to seek the shelter of the bracken on our side, from whence she sprang; so the poor fowl turned tail and 'went for it' in a long slanting descent from an incredible altitude. As they both neared us they presented the appearance of two little balls falling out of the sky right towards us, and quite straight, with the difference (fatal to the poor woodcock) that 'Taillie', who began below her, was now well above. The hawk was evidently unwilling or afraid to stoop over the water, but the moment the cock was over the land she shot herself forward, and straight in the air, instead of slanting, half perpendicular down, like her quarry (both moving with incredible speed), turned over, and stooped. No one knows the speed of a falcon's stoop, but it must be very great, as I have seen it bring a hawk up to old grouse flying hard downwind, just as though they had been sitting still, with absurd ease, if only she be but high enough. Anyhow, it was fatal this time to the woodcock, for, leaving a cloud of feathers behind, she tumbled head over heels before us into the very patch of bracken she came from, and meeting there with an old anthill, bounded off it many a yard and lay still. The hawk soon recovered herself, and dashed on to her well-earned quarry. Needless to say I did not disturb her thereon, but served out the whisky, and we drank her health all round. Then we too set to work at our lunch, and when this very tame pet hawk had nearly done hers, I went up to her and took her up, and having replaced the swivel in her jesses and the leash in her swivel, and cleaned her feet and wiped her beak and kissed her, I fastened her to a stone in a lonely burn close by, and witnessed her bathe and dry herself in the sun, preening her feathers to her and our entire satisfaction, and I trust to the satisfaction of the readers of my tale.

During his early years as a falconer, Major Fisher flew his hawks in Gloucestershire, in enclosed country not ideally suited to long-wing

Heron Hawking, an oil painting by E. Landseer.

hawking. In the fields around Coates and Tarlton near Cirencester and the wooded land near Sapperton, west of the great woodlands of Cirencester Park, Major Fisher and his servant would fly partridge and the occasional rook with eyass peregrines. With his pointer, Fan, who was outstanding at finding 'put-in' partridge, they had a deal of success, but then removed to South Wiltshire for partridge and rook and later to Northumberland for grouse hawking. Many good hawks were flown during this period: 'Blanche', an eyass falcon, excellent at partridge, who killed the first grouse for Major Fisher on the mountains at Bala, in North Wales, and 'Band of Hope' and 'Lundy', two eyass tiercels, both of whom came to untimely ends after years of faithful service. 'Band of Hope' was killed at Imber, on Salisbury Plain, by a ploughman with his ox-goad. The tiercel 'Lundy' was killed by a man with a hoe for killing a pigeon.

In 1877 'Band of Hope' and 'Lundy', then in their third season at partridge, together with an old eyass falcon and a young eyass falcon called 'Erin', took a total of 142 partridges on the downs near Chitterne in Wiltshire. The following season the two tiercels alone took 160 partridges. 'Erin', the eyass falcon of 1877, took only fourteen of the partridge scored in that year but also caught an old female sparrowhawk. It was Major Fisher's practise to form a line of his men, falconer, assistant falconer and cadgeman, with himself, mounted, in the centre of the line. The falcon would then be cast off to wait on over the men as they swept the stubble for partridge. While doing this with the eyass 'Erin', she suddenly raced away, ignoring all lures, and after some fine flying took the sparrowhawk, both falling into a patch of high rape. On making in to her, she was fed on something rather better, an old partridge killed earlier that day, replaced on the cadge, and taken home, so ending the day with a flight to be remembered.

With good passage hawks for the rook hawking and eyasses for partridge in September and October of each year, Major Fisher enjoyed the very best of falconry. Never really interested in the goshawk or the sparrowhawk, he concentrated his attention on peregrines, trying the occasional gyrfalcon when one came his way. Of course, not all of the passage peregrines trained for rook hawking entered well to that sable quarry. One such was a passage falcon of 1876 named 'Acrobat'. Not willing to take on rooks, Fisher gave her to his friend, the Rev W. Willimott, who successfully entered her to seagull and killed many of them near Veryan Bay in Cornwall.

Often falconers would help one another in obtaining hawks. Brodrick occasionally managed to get eyasses from Lundy for the Major, and Mr Evans, a falconer in Cambridge, sent a fine falcon to Stroud. Named 'Cuckoo' (not the nicest of names), she became a successful falcon in the field and a firm favourite with Major Fisher.

Of the many peregrines that were flown by Major Hawkins Fisher perhaps the best remembered is 'Lady Jane Grey', a passage falcon from Valkenswaard that was flown at grouse for eight seasons. Grouse hawking requires many ingredients, all equally necessary to ensure success. These ingredients Major Fisher had in a fine little moor, abundantly stocked with grouse, really good hawks and dogs, and the services of two very active, hardworking and competent falconers, James Rutford and his

The two falconers James Rutford and
Thomas Allen with the grouse hawks of
Major Fisher and Charles Radclyffe, 1897.

brother William. Of hawks, the Major had his share of good and bad
ones and, as he remarked at the end of the season of 1887, of the eight
peregrines of various ages that accompanied him to Riddlehamhope,
only four proved themselves at grouse. Of these four, two had had
previous experience, the intermewed passage falcon 'Lady Jane Grey'
and the intermewed eyass falcon 'Lundy'. The score for the season was:
'Lady Jane' – 44 grouse, 'Lundy' – 29, 'Dutch Lady' – 20, 'Princess' – 15
and a snipe, and 'Queen', a haggard falcon caught on the Wiltshire
Downs, 3 grouse only, she having a damaged foot, a total of 111 grouse.
The hawks went out altogether twenty-six times, their best days being: 20
August – 9 grouse, 19 September – 6, 20 September – 8, 22 September –
7. Only on four occasions did hawks spend a night out, not being found
on their kills, but all were taken up next morning and all the hawks
returned south on 6 October. At the end of his summary of the season
Major Fisher writes: *I must thank my neighbours for their kindness, my friend for
again placing so suitable a moor and comfortable abode at my service, and his keeper*

75

G.E. Lodge.

(*opposite*)   A Red Shahin falcon from a
gouache by G.E. Lodge. This falcon was the
property of Captain C. W. Thomson of the
7th Dragoon Guards.

Peregrine on Rook, an oil painting by G. E.
Lodge. 'Stratagem', a passage peregrine,
trapped in the autumn of 1893, caught a
total of 29 rooks and one jackdaw in 17 days
in the autumn of 1894.

The falconers and keeper, with hawks, at Riddlehamhope 1897

for believing the evidence which his senses daily afford him, that the constant flying of trained hawks on a most limited area, and on the same parts of that area, does not 'drive grouse off the ground'. I see little or no difference in their numbers to what they were at first, nor does the keeper either.

Late in the season, when grouse are wild and strong and fine birds, say, in October, the sport is at its best. We then make an extended line of five or six men abreast and sixty yards or so apart, the falconer with the hawk being usually in the centre. Just before the line starts in silence, he casts her off, and directly she is well aloft, a whistle or a wave of the hand and we all move on. A dog ranges wide, but is not much attended to, for, the birds being wild, he seldom gets much chance to point. (In the north of Scotland the grouse will lie to the point of a good dog well into November). Now is the time to see the grouse fly. Rising wild, and good at either cutting through a head wind, with driving wings and close compact body, or careering down it, their pace is terrific. A Yorkshire keeper, seeing for the first time a hooded hawk, laughed to scorn the idea of her catching a grouse. 'She canna speed the buds', quoth he; though she soon undeceived him as to this.

For forty-three years Major Charles Hawkins Fisher maintained a mews of falcons, and pursued the sport he loved so well. He died in 1901 and was buried on 30 October in the quiet churchyard at Stroud, with James Rutford, carrying a favourite falcon, standing at the graveside.

78

Sometimes critical of others, at least he was so with humour. Fond of writing in the margins of his books, some of his comments are distinctly cutting, as in Freeman and Salvin's book, **Falconry: Its Claims, History and Practice.** Freeman writes on page 115 of flying at partridge: 'We shall have to fly downwind I fear, but as there's scarcely any to fly down, it won't matter.' Fisher comments: 'You really never killed a partridge with a hawk in your life my friend — or you would never have written *that*! All *game* (rapid birds with short wings) *must* be *stooped at downwind* to kill, when they are wild and strong.' On page 177, where Freeman writes of losing his merlin from the damp, Major Fisher, presumably writing on a typical wet day, notes, 'Tis all "up" *then.* With all the falcon tribe!'

He also saw the humour of the situation when on one occasion he had to lead his horse home from rook hawking, the saddle being too wet to sit on. Having left the mare tethered, with the usual lead weight tied by a rein to the bit, as was the practise with falconers, he took some time lifting a young passage hawk from her kill. On looking for his horse he could see her nowhere until he searched in a hollow in the down. There, in a dew pond, the Major found his mare, thoroughly enjoying herself in deep and muddy water.

79

7
Major
Charles Radclyffe

Charles Robert Eustace Radclyffe was born in 1873, the eldest son of Charles James Radclyffe of Foxdenton Hall in Lancashire and Hyde House, Bere Regis, near Wareham, in Dorset. Few people have managed to pack as much sport into one life as did Major Radclyffe — hunting, shooting, fishing, big game hunting, boxing, breeding gundogs, exploring and falconry. Well he remembered what his father told him at the turn of the century, 'Mark my words. I have seen the best years of England, and you will never see the like again.' He did his best to prove his father wrong.

Charles Radclyffe started to shoot at the age of nine with an old 18-bore single-barrel muzzle-loader by the great Joe Manton, a gun that had been used as the beginner's gun in the family for many years. The young man's first success at a flying bird was a fine blackcock on the heaths at Hyde, where at that time blackgame were still quite numerous. His first salmon, a clean-run fish of thirty-three pounds, he took on a fly on the River Frome, by the kindness of Mr Merthyr Guest, who was for so long the Master of the Blackmore Vale hounds. Charles Radclyffe's earliest memories of hunting were with his grandfather, Mr C. J. R. Radclyffe. He had taken over the hounds of Mr J. Farquharson in 1858. The pack was kennelled at Hyde and was known as 'Mr Radclyffe's Hounds'. For some thirty years they hunted what is now the South Dorset country. When too old to ride to hounds Grandfather Radclyffe put a good hunter between the shafts of a hansom-cab, and in this, with his grandson as company, would career across country and rattle along narrow roads. Knowing the country well they often saw more of a run than those who were mounted on the best hunters.

In addition to this Major Radclyffe's father got together a pack of draft foxhounds with which he hunted roe-deer and at which he showed excellent sport.

Brought up in such an atmosphere, it is hardly surprising that Major Radclyffe became renowned for his sporting abilities. Quickly he learnt the correct way of carrying a gun and remembered all his life being put in his place by Colonel Napier Sturt, who had been walking behind him. Touching Radclyffe on the arm he said: 'Boy, I see you are shooting with No. 5 shot today.'

Radclyffe asked him how he knew. 'Because, since you have been

(*opposite*) 'Shadow of Death', a female goshawk, from an oil painting by G. E. Lodge. A fine goshawk flown for seven seasons by her owner, T. J. Mann, between 1886 and 1892.

Charles Radclyffe with the falcon 'Dover' at Riddlehamhope 1897

'Jack' Frost, falconer to Dr Arbel of Vadancourt in France

Grace Radclyffe with a young falcon 'Duchess' at Hyde 1898

carrying your gun for five minutes with the trigger guard on your shoulder, I have been looking down the barrel all the time. If you will only reverse your gun and carry it with the trigger guard uppermost, the tallest man in England would be safe if it went off.' So were such lessons taught and remembered.

As a young man of sixteen, Radclyffe started keeping hawks and for many years maintained the largest establishment of trained hawks in Europe, excepting the Old Hawking Club. His early mentor was Major Charles Hawkins Fisher, regarded by many as the greatest falconer of his day. For many years he hawked rooks on Salisbury Plain from Major Fisher's hawking lodge at Chitterne, and hawked grouse at Riddle-hamhope in Northumberland. In those days partridges were plentiful on the extensive grounds of the Radclyffe estate at Hyde. The open heather-clad moorland was scattered here and there with small patches of gorse bushes and furze and in the centre of the heath lay a few small cultivated fields which afforded good feeding for the partridges. Visiting this ground with falconers, a cadge of peregrines, a pointer and a couple of spaniels, they would beat out the farm fields to drive the partridge on to the open moor.

Tom Allen was head falconer to Major Radclyffe for many years. With a fine sense of humour, he was a good companion besides being a skilful falconer. In 1899 he travelled with Major Radclyffe to Spa in Belgium to compete in an international falconry contest. In order to add to the

82

attractions of the season at Spa, the committee of the Cercle des Etrangers, with the cooperation of the Société Royale de St Hubert of Belgium, announced an interesting *chasse au faucon* with prizes worth £160. Major Radclyffe was the first to enter and took over five peregrines: 'Black Lady', an intermewed eyass falcon, 'The Miller', an intermewed eyass tiercel, 'Bridport', an intermewed eyass falcon, 'Princess', a young eyass falcon and 'Dover', an intermewed falcon. His only opponent was Dr Arbel of the Château de Vadancourt in France. Dr Arbel, whose falconer was Jack Frost, brought three hawks with him, 'Sybille', a young eyass falcon, and two intermewed tiercels, 'Satan' and 'Cyrano de Bergerac'. As the game season had not opened the hawks were flown at pigeons. An excellent spot was chosen, about four miles from Spa, on the fine moors at Malchamps, the contest taking place on 19 August. The falconers and hawks were kindly housed by M. Herrfeldt at the Château de Marteau, and attracted much attention in the local villages. The judges were Colonel Westropp, Captain Fairfax-Adams and the Baron M. de Schauenburg. In the first flight 'The Princess' flew high over the falconer and caught her pigeon against the wind. Her opponent scored several points by her obedience but failed to kill.

'Black Lady', Major Radclyffe's favourite falcon

FIRST FLIGHT for 300 fr.
Mr C. E. Radclyffe's 'Princess'	1st
Dr Arbel's 'Sybille'	2nd

In the next flight 'Black Lady' met a difficult pigeon and failed to kill. 'Cyrano de Bergerac' also had a difficult pigeon, but he managed to kill after a very long flight.

SECOND FLIGHT for 400 fr.
Dr Arbel's 'Cyrano de Bergerac'	1st
Mr C. E. Radclyffe's 'Black Lady'	2nd

In the third flight 'Satan', flown first, stooped well but did not foot

Two of the most celebrated game hawks; the tiercel 'Killer', twelve years old, and the falcon 'Black Lady', five years old

Hawking in Hungary. After a kill. Richard Best, falconer, feeding a falcon on a partridge. In the carriage is Princess Odescalchi.

(opposite) Major Radclyffe with salmon from the River Frome. Taken on the fly, 4 April 1905: length 48½ inches, girth 24 inches, weight 41 lbs.

cleverly and after a long chase he lost the pigeon in a wood. 'Bridport' waited on high but her pigeon proved too strong and fast and beat her to the same wood.

THIRD FLIGHT for 600 fr.
Mr C. E. Radclyffe's 'Bridport'
Dr Arbel's 'Satan' divided

FOURTH FLIGHT for 200 fr.
Mr C. E. Radclyffe's 'Dover' flew over.

A lot of interest was shown in the contest and it was reported in **The Sporting Life, The Daily Mail, The Field** and in some European papers, some of which were not very accurate in their reporting. In one paper it noted: *'Il est des faucons qui ne manquent jamais leur oiseau, malgré les crochets que l'instinct fait faire à la victime. Ces faucons valent cinq à six mille francs.'* As Radclyffe noted in the margin, 'Nonsense'. Further on in the same report: *'M. Radclyffe, qui est un fervent de ce sport, parvient ainsi dans son domaine d'Ecosse à prendre 25 à 30 perdreaux en une bonne journée de chasse. Ses faucons, qui ne chassent que l'oiseau, auront ici à lutter contre des faucons élevés en France.'* Radclyffe comments, 'Absurd rot'.

About this time Tom Allen was responsible for training a few men to

84

be falconers. One of these men was Richard Best, who was trained as falconer to Colonel Gilbert Blaine (see Chapter VIII); another was Lightfoot who went over to Hungary as falconer to Prince Zoard Odescalchi. Major Radclyffe was responsible for sending over both Best and Lightfoot with a team of hawks, and so started yet another enthusiast on the road to success. Undoubtedly Hungary was ideally suited to hawking, with its many thousands of acres devoid of trees, open country well stocked with partridges, and in season multitudes of duck. After helping to get a good mews of hawks established and showing fine sport for a few seasons, Richard Best returned as full-time falconer to Gilbert Blaine.

Prior to Best and Lightfoot departing for Hungary in November, 1901, Radclyffe and Blaine had some excellent partridge hawking at Hyde and Wool Heath. Looking at Radclyffe's diary one sees they had a big team of hawks: 'Clawless', 'Tiny', 'Black Lady', 'Young Black Lady', 'Big Eye', 'Little John', 'Danceaway', 'Ready', 'The Miller', 'Black Queen' and others.

That autumn Colonel Blaine had decided to make 1901 his last season with his hawks in Dorset. Radclyffe was sorry about this as it was nice to have another falconer so near to his home. As the first day of that season fell on a Sunday, Radclyffe took the hawks out to Wareham Heath on Saturday, 31 August and bagged a brace of partridges with the tiercels. That evening he played in a cricket match at Wool and succeeded in making twenty-three runs, much to his surprise. On Monday, 2 September, despite it being a bad partridge season, the hawks took three and a half brace of which 'Black Lady', now in her eighth season, took three birds. An amusing entry for 23 September reports: *I took the hawks to Wool Heath and met Blaine at 11.30. We found a good lot of birds and bagged three*

Mrs Radclyffe with her record Norwegian salmon of 53½ lbs.

Major Radclyffe casting off the young falcon 'Danceaway'.

partridges and a landrail. I spent some time in the evening trying to catch the tiercel 'Ready', *which went off with a partridge and carried it all over the Warren Heath. I got the partridge but not the hawk which I left after much swearing in Black Castle fir trees.* The next day the comment: *I find that my acting falconer, Fred Lightfoot, is far inferior in energy to Tom Allen, although the former is younger by some fifteen years than the latter.* Tom Allen had been away in Belgium with another team of game hawks and, on his return, left two falcons there, a young one and old 'Danceaway'.

28 October. *I heard with the deepest regret that my old friend, Major Fisher of Stroud died on Saturday last at the age of 76 years. One of the kindest friends and best sportsmen that ever lived.*

2 November. *We only got two flights and bagged one with* 'Little John'. *This hawk is a very promising tiercel and one which I shall be sorry to part with although I must send him to Hungary shortly as I have promised to send Prince Odescalchi four hawks and cannot do so without this hawk goes.*

4 November. *A fine and calm day. We went to Wool Heath with the hawks and met Blaine there for our last combined day together, as Best and Lightfoot are leaving here on Wednesday and going to Hungary. This leaves Blaine with no falconer and me with very few hawks, so I conclude that our season is about over now.*

Lunch at Kalloway's Farm on Wool Heath, Dorset

Not content with hawking, shooting and fishing in England, and shooting and hawking in Hungary, Major Radclyffe and his wife went salmon fishing in Norway. Mrs Radclyffe caught a salmon of 53½ lbs on the Namsen. This fish was hooked and played for two hours, part from the boat and the rest of the time from the bank. A fisherman's dream, no doubt, but even in the Frome, that gentle Wessex river, Major Radclyffe caught a salmon of 41 lbs.

There is no doubt that Major Radclyffe was a big game hunter and traveller of great skill and experience, but many of his friends will remember him more as an avid letter writer to **The Field** and other papers. The subject matter ranged far and wide, 'The Breaking Of Dogs', 'Working and Show Retrievers', 'Hints for Grouse-Driving Late in the Season', 'Preservation of Big Game in South Africa', 'The "Calling" of Elk', 'The Territorial Army', 'Fishing in Iceland', 'The Hunted Otter', 'The Army and Ulster', and 'Fly and Bait', a controversy that went on for some months, getting rather more heated as time went by, finally producing a challenge from Major Radclyffe:

Fly and Bait

Sir, I note that 'West Country' has now launched a new line of attack on me in **The Field,** *and this time two other anonymous correspondents have been called in to his support.*

I notice that both 'West Country' and his friends are very free with their polite (?) terms for the various forms of complaints from which I am supposed to suffer; and therefore there is no reason why I should not reply in their own language, as I certainly hold strong views on their incorrect statements.

Mystery correspondent No. 1 in **The Field** *of 13 September begins well by admitting that he has not read the correspondence on the controversy into which he plunges. After a fairly accurate description of the River Forss, he proceeds to indulge in a few 'terminological inexactitudes'. He states that on all rivers north of Inverness you are told that 'Fly Only' is allowed. Also that we use vast 'Gobs of Fuzz' for flies. Now nothing could be further from the truth as regards the River Forss.*

In the first place I have made a rule here for more than 20 years on this river that if they like to butcher small salmon on strong traces, and stiff rods, with triangles of hooks and baits, my friends may do so. But here where we fish with the finest of casts, and the smallest and lightest dressed flies possible to find, we prefer to kill salmon in what we consider a sportsmanlike and gentlemanly manner.

Hawking Party, Dorset 1899

89

Correspondent No. 1 also states that he should 'expect to do better here with bait than with fly'. In conclusion I can only say that I will give him a chance to try it on any good fishing days in April and May, and will bet him a 'fiver' each day that I beat his bag using a 'Fly Only'.

Yours faithfully,
C. E. Radclyffe.

Forss House,
Thurso, N.B.

It would appear that the challenge was never accepted.

Another controversy developed over the origins of the yellow Labrador, Miss E. V. Buller claiming that Mrs Hurt's statement that all yellow Labradors were descended from the Hyde or Knaith kennels was incorrect. Back came Major Radclyffe's reply:

Yellow Labradors

Sir, I read with interest the letter in **The Field** *of 15 February. It is rather difficult to understand what the writer means when speaking of tracing the ancestors of a yellow Labrador back to 1896. Does this mean that the owners claim there were any yellow Labradors in England in that year, except those in my kennels at Hyde? If so, I can assure them they are wrong.*

Major Radclyffe at Hyde, October, 1901.

It is true, there were many flat-coated yellow retrievers in England before 1896, such as those owned by Lord Ilchester, Lord Tweedmouth, and others; and a number of so-called yellow Labradors today are descended from some of these dogs. That is why, in my opinion, we see so many Labradors today with wrong coats, and quite different in many ways from the original so-called Labradors.

I should be interested to know the name of Tawton Burd's first yellow ancestor, when it was born, and the name of its owner. I could then probably help by saying how this freak arose.

All the yellow Labradors owned by my friends Major and Mrs Wormald at Knaith were originally descended from Ben of Hyde. The same applies to the kennels of Colonel R. Swan, and Mr G. Atkinson Clarke and a few others who helped early in 1900 to found and establish this new type of dog.

The pedigrees of my dogs at Hyde go back far beyond 1896, but it was not till late in the 'nineties that I ever saw or heard of a yellow Labrador, and then two were born in the same litter from black parents.

Yours faithfully,
C. E. Radclyffe (Major).

Hyde, Wareham.

Another regular subject for comment was the varying speeds of birds in flight.

The Speed of Birds

Sir, I noticed in The Field *of 12 June the often discussed subject of the speed of birds had been revived once more, and this time by no less an authority than Mr F.W. Frohawk. It is rather astonishing to see that he says: 'It is known that the ordinary flight of teal is 150 m.p.h.'*

I wonder how this speed has been discovered and proved. It is, I think, generally admitted that the peregrine falcon is the swiftest flyer amongst our British birds. Now, speaking as a falconer of many years experience, I, and several other falconers, have found that the maximum speed of peregrines to be from 100 to 120 miles per hour, and at this speed they can overhaul and catch other birds. As regards teal, peregrines can overhaul and catch them with the greatest ease, and I have killed many of them with good tiercels.

The ordinary mallard, however, is much faster than a teal when pursued by falcons. I have constantly flown hawks at flocks of ducks and teal mixed, and the former have always flown clean away from the teal when both are going at the top speed to escape their pursuer...

The above letter was dated 18 September, 1943, and produced as much interest as the same subject had in **The Observer** in 1921 and in **The Field** in 1922. Then the overall opinion had been that in level flight the peregrines rarely exceeded 65 m.p.h. but in the stoop could possibly reach as high as 120 m.p.h. It was also generally agreed that although the teal was able to get into top gear more quickly, the mallard, indeed, was the faster bird.

One more subject for discussion was the height at which game can be killed with a shotgun.

High Pheasants

Sir, I have read recently in **The Field** *letters claiming that pheasants can be killed, presumably with an ordinary game gun, at heights up to 200 ft.*

Now if anyone thinks that this can be done, I would ask them to go and look at the Duke of York's Column in London. This is, I believe, exactly 120 ft, or 40 yards high.

The London pigeons can often be seen flying from the top of the monument. If a man killed one of them he would, I think, write pages about it. But let him add another 80 ft or two-thirds more to the height of the monument, which would make his bird about 67 yds above his head. Is there any reputable game shot today who would even raise his gun to a pheasant passing this height overhead? If I saw him shooting at such a bird, he would certainly never be invited by me to one of my shoots...

Perhaps the last paragraph of the next letter should be noted.

Snipe Averages

Sir, With regard to the recent correspondence in your columns on the subject of snipe averages, I recall an occasion several years ago when I was shooting snipe in Southern Spain with Major C. E. Radclyffe, who was undoubtedly the finest shot I have ever seen. On the occasion of which I write the snipe were not particularly plentiful, but we flushed a fair number during the course of the day.

Any bird which came within range of Major Radclyffe's gun was as good as dead before he had even raised his gun to his shoulder. About 15 to 20 snipe were shot that day, all of which fell to Major Radclyffe's gun, my contribution being one 'probable'. I could not swear to this, but I am pretty certain that he did not have a single miss.

There was one shot in particular which I remember. It was during the course of a drive and a single bird came directly over Major Radclyffe's head, well out of range, or so I thought. But I was mistaken, for he literally 'pulled it out of the sky' and it fell at his feet.

Government House
Gibraltar.

> *Yours faithfully,*
> *H. D. Barry (Captain)*

The tattooed back of Major C. E. Radclyffe

In many of Radclyffe's diaries the entry often occurs: 'I spent the day writing letters'. A man of many talents he enjoyed life with rod, gun, hawk or pen, and helped many others to enjoy his pleasures. Such a long and varied career in many lands provided Major Radclyffe with a fund of sporting tales but one which amused the Major in his hawking days should perhaps be included here. Evidently the falconers proved an attraction to the local village lasses wherever they went and well Radclyffe remembered one morning at Tilshead on the Plain. As the falconers were seen approaching, an old woman called out to her daughter, who was smiling at the falconers from the garden: 'Come in, our Sue, here come they hawkers agen. They don't care whose daughters they be arter. They be here today and gone tomorrer! Come in, our Sue.'

One last instance of Major Radclyffe's enthusiastic extremes is best illustrated by a look at his bare back. There tattooed by that master of the craft, Sutherland MacDonald, is a flying falcon about to foot a partridge from a covey going for cover around to the front! Turn the Major around and there emblazoned right across his chest was the Radclyffe coat-of-arms. In 1904 a photograph of the Major's chest plus coat-of-arms appeared in a New York paper with the comment that, 'It had remained a secret until his death, which took place recently in South Africa.' This newspaper cutting appears in Radclyffe's own scrap book under the heading in his own handwriting, 'A Premature Obituary Notice', to which he added, 'It is not granted to all of us that we may read an account of our own death, and still be in the land of the living.'

(opposite) Major Charles Eustace Radclyffe of Hyde, Dorset

Gilbert Blaine watching Radclyffe flying his
favourite old falcon, 'Black Lady'

8
Captain Gilbert Blaine

Just as Edward Clough Newcome, the most skilful amateur falconer of his time, had kept falconry alive through the ten years or so that separated the closure of the Loo Hawking Club and the start of rook hawking on the Plain, so Captain Gilbert Blaine, without question the most skilful falconer of his day, was the link between the last of the Old Hawking Club and the infancy of the falconry of today.

A protegé of Major Fisher, Blaine started hawking in the last years of the nineteenth century. His first real successes were at partridge hawking which he practised with Major Radclyffe on the latter's estates in Dorset. At that time Blaine rented a small house with a walled garden known as The Cottage at Bere Regis, and there he started in a small way with four tiercels. Before very long, with his falconer Richard Best, he began to achieve the sort of results in game hawking that clearly showed Blaine's complete understanding of the sport. In 1899, with James Rutford and four of Major Fisher's falcons to make up the team, Blaine took a total of 102 partridges and ten sundries. Blaine's tiercels were 'Lulworth', an intermewed eyass tiercel, 'Ready', an intermewed passage tiercel, 'Lucifer' (from Dover) and 'Black Jack', two eyass tiercels. Two pointers, Drake and Dido, helped by the spaniel Boss, were the dogs used. Undoubtedly the most successful of the tiercels was 'Ready', who took forty-five of the total scored.

In 1900, now with a team of six hawks of his own, Blaine improved by one his score of the previous year. Among his hawks was 'Lundy', the first of the many peregrines that he obtained from the island over the next twenty-five years. Indeed perhaps this tiercel was the very reason for Blaine's determination to get Lundy peregrines, for in his first season this lovely little tiercel killed the top score of fifty-six partridges, bettering by fourteen the score of the experienced old passage tiercel, 'Ready'. One other innovation that year was the addition of a setter bitch to his kennel of bird dogs. In 1901, hoping no doubt to add more stars to his team, Blaine managed to get three eyasses from Lundy, but, taken far too young, they all came to nothing. However, the old Lundy tiercel kept up his good work and killed forty-two partridges, still sharing the cadge with the old passage tiercel 'Ready' and a newly acquired passage tiercel 'Robin'. Writing of his first Lundy tiercel Blaine said of him: *He was of slender build, a lovely head and large feet; he was at hack for five weeks. When*

The Fiat car, specially designed to carry hawks

95

'Black Cloud', a young Lundy tiercel of 1908. A fine partridge hawk

entered to quarry he did not, at first, go high, no doubt relying on his great speed and clever footing. Later in the season he waited on high and for upwards of half an hour at a time, and would not come down until he had killed.

It wasn't until 1907 that Gilbert Blaine obtained further Lundy eyasses that were of outstanding merit. That year two falcons and a tiercel were put out to hack. Left out perhaps too long, one of the falcons was lost, but after nearly six weeks the other two were taken up, the tiercel 'Lundy III' proving to be a game hawk of outstanding excellence at partridge and later at grouse through eight seasons. By this time Blaine had left the heathlands of Dorset and had rented a partridge manor on the Berkshire Downs and from there moved on to the open downland surrounding Tilshead where he flew hawks annually until 1912.

By 1908 the whole team of game hawks were Lundy eyasses: 'Lundy III' and 'Olive', the falcon, intermewed, and three eyass tiercels, brothers, named 'Lundy IV', 'Castaway' and 'Black Cloud'. This team of hawks put up the fine score of 296 head.

By now transport had progressed from the pony and four-wheel brake of Dorset days to a specially adapted Fiat touring car. With the tonneau removed there was still not sufficient shelter and room for the hawks, so the combined inventive abilities of chauffeur and falconer were called into play. A seat was built out at the back, like the rear seat on a horse-drawn dog cart, with a wide footboard overhanging the petrol tank, and detachable sidepieces joined the two wings to the sides of the reversed seat. Left, therefore, between the driver's seat and the rear-facing seat, was a sheltered level platform where the hawk box cadge could be transported. This car on occasions was known to have transported the driver and two passengers in the front seat, two on the rear seat, one on each step (what would the police say today?), five peregrines on the box cadge with three merlins on a smaller box cadge set inside the larger one, three dogs, the field cadge and the luncheon basket.

Blaine's custom was to drive the partridge from the open downland, where the lack of cover made it difficult to get up to the birds, into the turnip fields, which at that time were grown for the large flocks of sheep found in downland country. But let Blaine describe a day: *We disembark and station ourselves under cover of the hedge, and in a minute or two the shrill note of a whistle announces that some partridges have been flushed; in another moment a small covey of five comes skimming low over a bare piece of ploughed land, and drops into the lower end of the roots. As soon as the men have come up, we form a line along the upper side of the roots at intervals of about ten yards. The falconer takes 'Black Cloud' on hand, as he can generally be trusted to fly steadily early in the day, and the warm sun and light wind may tempt the other hawks to soar. His leash and swivel, and lastly the hood, are removed, and the tiercel, after taking a comprehensive glance at our dispositions, launches himself into the air, and skims away low along the line. We all keep still to give the hawk time to get up to his pitch, which he attains very rapidly, not in circles, but by taking a long beat against the wind nearly down to the village, half a mile away.*

One of the ladies, watching his rapidly diminishing outline, expresses a fear that we have seen the last of him; but the initiated show no signs of apprehension, and she is soon reassured by seeing the hawk turn and come rapidly back high overhead. The red setter is allowed to run, and we all move forward while she ranges through the roots

96

ahead of the line. The tiercel, meanwhile, is circling high overhead and still rising. The setter has got a line, and is drawing on steadily, but has not come to a stand yet. The birds are evidently running in front of her down the drills. At this moment, a thrush rises with a shriek at the feet of one of the party and flips along aimlessly over the root tops. The tiercel is right over and cannot resist the temptation. He falls headlong from his pitch with a whirr and a rush just behind the thrush, skims on like a flash, and passing over it, leaves a cloud of soft feathers in his track, while the victim falls audibly plump among the green. Someone runs forward and picks it up stone dead as the tiercel throws up from his stoop and turns to recover his prey. Meanwhile we must hold hard a moment to let him mount to his pitch again. He has risen spirally to half the height from which he fell, and as he is making another ring the partridges spring up in front of the dog at the lower corner of the roots and whizz away downhill at their best pace, towards the shelter of the little meadow that adjoins the village. The tiercel is round and into line in an instant, and follows in hot pursuit. He is nearly 200 yards behind them, and they have half a mile to fly to cover.

It is a stern chase; the partridges soon fade from view, but the hawk is still visible, cleaving through the air with rapid and machine-like strokes of his wings. He rises obliquely as he goes, and then descends rapidly and disappears below the brow. The falconer follows in the line of flight while the rest wait in their places.

In a few minutes he returns with the tiercel hooded, holding a headless partridge by the legs. 'Where did he kill?' someone asks him. 'Fifty yards short of the hedge in the bottom,' is the reply.

This was on Wednesday, 28 October, 1908. The bag for that day was: 'Lundy III' two partridges, 'Black Cloud' two partridges and the thrush, 'Lundy IV' two partridges, and 'Castaway' a single partridge. A total of seven partridges and one thrush in ten flights.

At the end of the season Gilbert Blaine gave the intermewed falcon

'Lundy V', an eyass tiercel of 1909

(opposite above) 'Antoinette', a passage falcon belonging to Gilbert Blaine. A fine partridge hawk, in 1909 she accounted for 77 partridge and only missed 4 during the season

(opposite below) 'Lundy IV', an eyass peregrine tiercel, the property of Gilbert Blaine. He accounted for 18 grouse, 274 partridge and 19 various between 1908 and 1912

'Olive' to the Old Hawking Club, and for some seasons she continued to fly partridge in George Oxer's capable hands at Avebury on the partridge shoot of Charles Garnett, a one-time member of the Old Hawking Club.

The following season Blaine again had four Lundy tiercels in his team, 'Castaway' being replaced by an eyass of that year, 'Lundy V'. By the end of the first month these tiercels had brought to bag a total of 135 partridges, 'Lundy III' – 37, 'Lundy IV' – 32, 'Black Cloud' – 31, and the new tiercel, 'Lundy V' – 35. By the end of the season the total was 310 partridges. Sadly, the brilliant eyass 'Lundy V' was lost before the end of the season. Blaine wrote in his diary at the end of that season, *'May they fly as bravely and well next season as they have done this. There is no fault to be found with their work, which has been as consistently good as man could wish to see.'*

In the autumn of 1909 a beautiful little tiercel, 'shaped like a swift', was captured in Ireland and sent to Blaine. Within six weeks 'Gnome', for so he was called in honour of 'the little people', killed his first partridge. This tiercel was put up to moult with the Lundy tiercels and Blaine opened the 1910 season with 'Lundy III', 'Lundy IV' and 'Gnome', also an intermewed passage falcon, 'Antoinette', who had killed a few partridge the previous season. For the first ten days of the season Blaine was joined by 'Jack' Frost, who had a falcon and a tiercel which accounted for sixteen partridge, Blaine's four hawks bringing the total to 330 head. The highest score of his four hawks was that of 'Lundy IV', who killed eighty-three, and the lowest that of 'Gnome' with seventy-two to his credit. This little hawk was suffering from bad corns, and it was only at the end of October that a large one was extracted from the ball of his right foot. This probably was the reason why he very rarely trussed a partridge, but nearly always cut them down and then had to scramble on the ground for them.

That year Blaine bought a very useful English setter at Aldridge's. Bred by Captain Heywood-Lonsdale, Ightfield Griffin became very useful by the end of the season and played a large part in the breeding of many of the setters in Blaine's famous 'Westdown' kennels.

On one occasion that year 'Old Lundy' disappeared. After a long search Blaine found him sitting on a stunted thorn bush. As he approached a few partridge rose close to the tiercel, who made no attempt to chase them. Blaine then found that one of the jesses had become entangled on a thorn. He released him and put him up over the bush when, on a kick being administered to the base of the bush, out flew a partridge.

Each year Gilbert Blaine's successes at partridges improved and 1911, his last season on Salisbury Plain, was no exception. The summer had been exceptionally hot and dry and owing to this there was very little cover on the plain. The harvest was carried a month earlier than usual and partridge were thought to be few and far between. Eight eyasses were hacked at Tilshead Lodge of which five were taken up and trained; of these two turned out well.

Small individual happenings make most days memorable when out with hawks, some pleasing, some exciting and some disappointing. Blaine often noted such things in his diaries and reading of them brings those happenings very much to life.

6 September. *About twenty stone-curlew got up on a bare bit of ground when 'Lundy IV' was flying; he went into them and picked up one in his foot, but dropped it again. 'Gnome' would not fly. He is not fit, and constantly went to a tree to sit up. I think he is full of internal fat.*

9 September. *'Lundy IV' flew brilliantly and killed a peewit his second flight, after stooping at it three times and driving it to the ground where he sat on it.*

19 September. *'Sceptre' showed her long-hidden form today. She mounted twice magnificently, flying in the grand style of a wild falcon, and killed in two crashing stoops. The second bird she struck to the ground, making a cloud of dust fly, and never moved after she hit it.*

'Gnome' flown once, caught a hen sparrowhawk that had just finished eating a small bird and lucklessly rose beneath him. He struck her hard in his first stoop, then dusted her again and caught her as she attempted to put into gorse. We saved her life and took her home. 'Gnome' then killed a partridge. (The sparrowhawk was trained and killed five thrushes and blackbirds between 6 and 12 December).

12 October. *A curious incident occurred this morning in which 'Margherita' and 'Sceptre', being each flown in quick succession, each killed a partridge in the Orcheston Down valley, and were found sitting in the track not 20 yards from each other side by side.*

20 October. *A remarkable day for the number of different hawks seen, which included:*

1.   A buzzard being mobbed by rooks.
2.   A beautiful male Montagu's harrier.
3.   A peregrine tiercel.
4.   A pair of merlins or sparrowhawks.
5.   A merlin that played with 'Sceptre' when soaring.

27 October. *'Lundy IV' (lost on the 25th) was brought in by William at lunchtime. He had been caught by a carter at Chitterne who snared him by his whip lash on a partridge and took him home. The tiercel had been waiting on persistently over a party of people who were coursing hare, finally being rewarded by their putting up a covey for him when he stooped and had one immediately.*

7 November. *The brown spaniel chased 'Gnome' with the partridge in his foot clean out of sight!*

At the end of the season of 1912 Gilbert Blaine noted:

As compared with partridge hawking grouse hawking is in most aspects superior.

Where in Wiltshire, setters are of very little use in finding partridges for hawks, on a moor they are indispensable. No driving is necessary at all, for save in one or two places near farmsteads, into which grouse have a habit of 'putting in', a hawk can be flown wherever a dog gets a point. Then, when a 'put in' occurs, the grouse can always be found again, provided that the place is accurately marked, and flushed by a spaniel.

Grouse hardly ever run after putting in. I'm not sure that present day falconers would entirely agree with the last point

The great drawback was the habit the grouse had of throwing themselves down as soon as a hawk's stoop had brought her up to them. They would then get up and fly upwind at their best pace. The hawk had then no alternative but to course down the grouse in a long stern chase, in which half a mile or more was generally covered.

Grouse are much more difficult to catch than partridges, and try a hawk much more highly. A hawk needs to have been flying constantly and to be very fit and in high condition to catch grouse in October.

In August, perhaps for the first ten days, they are more easily killed than the smaller

Gilbert Blaine and party, partridge hawking on Salisbury Plain in 1908

and more active quarry. But after that period, their greater strength and power of sustained flight, and their wonderful speed in flying upwind tax the powers of even first class falcons to the utmost. Tiercels cannot fly them down going upwind at all.

Thus did Blaine sum up grouse hawking after his first real attempt at them. The hawks were sent up from Wiltshire to Barrogill Lodge at Mey in Caithness, on 2 August. The cadge consisted of the two old Lundy tiercels, Nos III and IV, 'Gnome', the old passage tiercel, and 'Margherita', the intermewed falcon from Orkney. All were a little backward in their moult, having spent the summer in a good dry loft over the stables at Shrewton. Five eyasses, all from Lundy, though from two separate eyries, were hacked, and of these a tiercel, 'Lundy VI', and his two sisters, from the east coast eyrie, were kept, and a falcon from the west coast of the island, the other falcon from that eyrie being sent to the Old Hawking Club.

Of the young hawks the two sisters 'Anna Pavlova' and 'Barbara' showed great promise and 'Anna' very soon learnt to mount and wait on, and developed the excellent habit of keeping upwind. 'Barbara' was not so steady at first, but was faster and more determined and by the end of the season improved into a wide-ranging and high-mounting falcon of the highest class. 'Mary Courtney', the third eyass falcon, was not in the same class as the other two, was backward in learning to wait on and was generally at a disadvantage when grouse rose through being a long way downwind. She was not a nice hawk to handle, being hot-tempered, but made great improvement during October. 'Lundy III' flew as well as ever he did at partridge and caught grouse right into October, which very few tiercels are capable of doing.

The three English setters used with the hawks were the dog **Griffin,** and **Belle** and **Glee,** bitches, who did wonderful work and, as Blaine noted, if it had not been for the excellence of their work, the hawks would never have done so well.

A total of 244 grouse were taken in thirty-eight days flying. This excellent score was noted in articles in **The Field** and **The Country**

Gentleman's Newspaper. One report, on the excellence of the setters used, was dated 21 September: *It is pleasing to hear that Mr Gilbert Blaine and his friends have had especially good sport over hawks at far-away Mey, and also that some of the best work in finding the game has been done by field-trial bred English setters handled by J. Frost, who, it will be well remembered, ran first and second in the Kennel Club Derby a few seasons since with a brace of puppies broken by and handled by his brother, Charles Frost. Mr Blaine's regular falconer returned from Hungary last season, and he now has the task of flying the hawks, his colleague, Frost, using the dogs, and between them uncommonly good sport has been provided for the Mey party. In a little over a fortnight from the beginning of the season, thirty-seven brace of grouse had been killed entirely by hawking, and it is worth recording that more than two-thirds of the flights were over a puppy of which Frost has the very highest opinion. One cannot wonder at that, for her game-finding abilities are said to be remarkable.*

Another article came from the pen of the Hon Gerald Lascelles, Secretary and Manager of the Old Hawking Club:

Mr Blaine is also a member (of the Old Hawking Club), but his hawks were trained by his own falconer, Best, and his own setters were worked by John Frost, well known as a successful handler at field trials. The Mey shootings in Caithness on the Pentland Firth were taken by Mr Blaine mainly for the purpose of hawking, and the shooting on those excellent moors — ideal for the purpose of hawking — was subordinated to the older sport. Hence the happy result which I think constitutes a record in the annals of grouse hawking, though never in my knowledge was it pursued under circumstances so favourable.

Mr Blaine was favoured beyond most mortals in obtaining three first-class eyass falcons of the year all of which made great scores. Most people think themselves fortunate if they only have one such falcon in any year. To this the principal part of the success is due. But he also had three first-class old tiercels which had killed a great number of partridges, and for high mounting and steadiness left nothing to be desired. But like most tiercels they fell off as grouse grew stronger, and though one of them especially killed grouse even in October it was found (as many others have found before) that it is to falcons that we must look for continued success with so powerful a quarry as grouse.

I have only known two or three tiercels that could kill grouse right through the

Falcon on partridge

season as well as a falcon. One especially I call to mind who performed this feat for two or three consecutive seasons,[1] but such hawks are very exceptional, and as a rule after about 10 September the tiercel cannot be relied on like his stronger sister.

Well may Blaine's successes of 1912 be acclaimed as a record grouse score. Certainly nowhere in the recorded history of the sport had more than one hundred brace of grouse been taken with a team of hawks in one season. However, the season of 1913 far surpassed this total and set a record of 406 grouse, a total unlikely to be ever beaten.

Nine young hawks were hacked in Wiltshire, four tiercels and five falcons. A nest from Lundy produced two tiercels and one falcon, three clutches came from Dover, and all had three weeks' hack. Of these only three falcons were kept, 'Sylvia', the Lundy falcon, 'Nora' and 'Dover II', both from Dover. The establishment was now very large indeed: two

Blaine, Radclyffe and Vivia Radclyffe

[1] This was 'Persimmon'. An eyass tiercel of 1897, he was from Donegal in Ireland.

falconers, Richard Best and his assistant of some years, Ted Woods; a new dog handler to replace Frost, a Mr J. S. Morris; a team of thirteen English setters and three spaniels, and the cadge of eight peregrines, six falcons and two tiercels:

'Lundy III'	Eyass tiercel	6 yrs
'Gnome'	Passage tiercel	4 yrs
'Anna Pavlova'	Eyass falcon	1 yr
'Barbara'	Eyass falcon	1 yr
'Gladys'	Passage falcon	1 yr
'Sylvia'	Eyass falcon	Young
'Nora'	Eyass falcon	Young
'Dover II'	Eyass falcon	Young

Gilbert Blaine. Blaine carried his hawks on his right hand, unlike the usual practise in the west.

This team of hawks, although putting together the highest score ever at grouse, were not by any means all stars but of course the best of them were very good indeed.

The moorland over which the hawks were flown extends to about nine thousand acres and is very flat, making it ideal for falconry, the major drawback being the fair scattering of crofts with their accompanying fenced fields and buildings to which the grouse invariably turn for refuge. Undoubtedly the most favourable condition of 1913 was the continuous spell of fine calm weather, the finest in the memory of the locals, that made it possible to make such a remarkable score.

In contrast to 1912 grouse were none too plentiful at the opening of the season, owing to the dryness of the moor, but more grouse appeared to move in as some rain improved the conditions. An interesting comment was that the grouse were not to be found in their favoured haunts of the previous year but in those places where none had been found.

20 August. 'Gnome', *after soaring and playing with a wild falcon came up at a great pitch and fell onto an old cock grouse, cutting it down with a broken wing.*

25 August. *The passage falcon as usual refused to mount and after coursing and putting in a grouse, caught a rook. We have given up all idea of flying her at game.*

6 September. *The game hawks all flew splendidly and killed 6 brace between 3 and 6.30. Grouse were sitting well and old Ranger got eight points in one place, each bird being killed in quick succession.*

22 September. *A grouse at which* 'Nora' *stooped jerked itself up in the air just as she came up to it and the falcon passed underneath it. This action on the part of the grouse is described in Major Fisher's book, but I have never seen it done before by a Caithness grouse.*

17 October. *Five brace, thus making our 200th brace of grouse killed by the hawks.*

In his summary of the season Gilbert Blaine commented that 'Sylvia' proved a very superior game hawk, making an unbroken run of forty-four grouse and a partridge without a miss, and topping the score for the season by killing ninety grouse and three sundries in ninety-three flights. This splendid falcon possessed all the qualities essential to the making of a perfect game hawk. She combined a calm and tractable disposition with keenness and perserverance in hunting, and a natural tendency to mount high with great speed and driving power at the end of the stoop.

103

'Gnome', a passage peregrine tiercel, 1909-13. His total score was 147 partridge, 61 grouse and 7 various

Of the old falcons 'Barbara', with her wonderful speed and the experience of a previous season, proved a very deadly hawk. She was always in earnest and strained every nerve to catch grouse. Very few escaped her and if she put them in at a distance she would hunt without assistance and often had the grouse in her foot when anyone got up to help her.

The old tiercel, 'Lundy III', then in his seventh season, held his own with the falcons right into October, and bowled over grouse after grouse in the brilliant style that had always made him the prime favourite with those who had seen him go through the performance. He was never put on the wing until late in the afternoon, when he could be relied upon to do his best, and he never failed us. 'Gnome' also acquitted himself well, and his style was much admired by the initiated.

A dog for grouse hawking should be a game finder, a fast and free ranger, and very staunch, and his nose should be so fine that he should never be guilty of making a false point, which is equivalent to saying that only those of the very highest class should ever be worked in conjunction with hawks. He should also excel in the qualities of discretion and self reliance. For it frequently happens that a dog is kept standing a long time on point while a falcon is mounting to her pitch, when grouse will take the opportunity of creeping away, sometimes passing out of wind of the dog and getting behind him. As soon as the hawk comes well overhead and is steady, the dog is required to cast for himself again and find them quickly. This a clever and experienced hand will often accomplish in a single cast.

The following table gives the score of grouse and sundries killed by Blaine's hawks in 1913.

	Grouse	Sundries	Unsuccessful Flights	Not Served	Total Times Flown
'Lundy III'	53	4	9	5	81
'Gnome'	41	9	12	3	65
'Anna Pavlova'	51	—	19	6	76
'Barbara'	80	—	12	5	97
'Sylvia'	90	3	2	5	100
'Norah'	81	1	9	1	92
'Gladys'	7	2	3	1	13
'Dover II'	3	—	1	—	4
	—	—			
	406	19			

How could any falconer follow up a year such as 1913? Was it possible to kill even more grouse in one season? Certainly Blaine noted in his diary that grouse appeared to be more plentiful than the previous season. 'Gnome', the old passage tiercel, had died and a new Lundy tiercel, hacked at Shrewton, was trained along with his sister and a Dover falcon. For the grouse season Blaine was lent an intermewed eyass falcon named 'Eva'. The property of the Old Hawking Club, she had a great reputation as a game hawk. She did not impress Blaine at first. **12 August**. 'Eva' *mounted well and killed, but was very slow at turning and getting onto her grouse quickly.* **13 August:** 'Eva', *being overkeen, crabbed no less than three separate hawks on the cadge. She appears to have the manners of a goshawk,*

One of Captain Blaine's 'Westdown' English setters

and is certainly not safe near other peregrines. **15 August:** '*Eva*' *is very fast and stoops hard, but does not hold her wings well.* [Blaine seems determined not to like her.] **20 August:** '*Eva*', *the Club falcon especially distinguished herself. She is a grouse hawk of the highest class, and has great drive and power in her stoop.* **17 September:** '*Eva*' *went magnificently twice and killed a brace. This falcon has the grand style and goes out very wide when mounting, coming overhead at a great pitch. She stoops very hard and rarely trusses but generally contents herself with cutting the grouse over, mounting again at once to deliver another blow from a high pitch, if necessary.*

So do opinions change of a hawk as the season progresses.

1914 did not turn out to be another record year. War intervened and Blaine was away much of the season in London. Best continued to fly the hawks and they ended the season with a total of 222 grouse. 'Sylvia', the star of the previous year, suffered throughout the season with 'croaks' but improved towards the end and flew with more vigour. The young Lundy falcon took some time to learn the game but eventually went high and kept well over and was very deadly at killing.

Nothing appears in Gilbert Blaine's hawking diaries until 1920. In that year he picked up the threads and returned to Caithness with a fresh team of hawks and setters. In fact Best had flown a small team of the old hawks at Barrogill in 1915, and had also entered a fine passage falcon of

the Old Hawking Club. This falcon, although heavy in the moult, proved as perfect a game hawk as could be found. She, and all the other old hawks, including the gallant little tiercel, 'Lundy III', died during the war in the moulting loft at Shrewton.

In September, 1919, Richard Best flew two young eyass falcons of Blaine's at partridges on the Wiltshire downs near Tilshead, in conjunction with Major Stanley Allen's hawks. One of these falcons, from Orkney, was moulted and taken to Caithness with two young passage falcons that had been flown at rooks in the spring on Salisbury Plain, and two young eyass falcons. So grouse hawking began again in 1920, now at Camster, a charming little moor, with a grey stone lodge that Blaine added to, to house his staff, with Blaine's partner, Captain Kenneth Palmer, renting the adjoining moors of Rowens, Badlibster and Scoriclate, land running right down to Strath and across to Stirkoke.

By 17 August 'Lady Jane', the smaller of the two moulting passage hawks, showed signs of understanding that grouse were being put up for her to the setter's point. 'White Wings', a large light-coloured falcon, who had refused rooks in the spring, took longer to get fit and to learn to wait on. In her first season at grouse 'Lady Jane' was inclined to visit the country for many miles around. Luckily on one occasion when she waited on over a neighbouring shooting party at Kensary, Blaine himself was one of the guns, having left Best to fly the falcons, so he took her down to a dead grouse.

By the middle of the season both falcons were going well and showed what the best of passage falcons were capable of.

21 September. 'Lady Jane', *flown twice, soared almost out of sight, then came over and from a great pitch cut over an old cock grouse in the valley by the Camster Burn.*

23 September. 'Lady Jane', *keeping well upwind of Free's point, cut a grouse over, apparently stone dead. Flown again, she was beaten by a pack of grouse going upwind. Coming back, another lot were found and I got her placed well upwind of these. When flushed, some turned up and some downwind. She stooped at an upwind one, and so lost her advantage, and as she was driving after it a beautiful old wild falcon came close by us like a streak of lightning, and flashed on after the grouse, passing* 'Lady Jane' *without an effort. She put the grouse into a gully and threw up,* 'Lady Jane' *coming on behind her and trying to sit on it.*

27 September. 'White Wings' *was joined by a wild falcon, the same old falcon that we see nearly every day. This falcon came up and waited on, beautifully placed upwind of the dog, and I urged Morris to go in and put up the grouse. He, however, did not understand what was wanted, seeing that* 'White Wings' *was at the time low and badly placed, and so a grand opportunity of seeing a wild falcon actually waiting on over a dog's point and stooping at a grouse flushed for her was missed.*

The falcon passed downwind right overhead, and the grouse, two, were flushed too late, and tore away into the wind and across the open ground to the N of the Shepherd's House. The wild falcon instantly gave chase and overhauled the grouse, that had at least 300 yards start of her, with incredible speed. 'White Wings', *seeing the hunt, came in from the right, and they passed out of sight. Soon after screaming was heard as of two hawks fighting, and* 'White Wings' *was finally picked up on a grouse about half a mile upwind.*

1 October: *Received a letter from M. P. A. Pichot, sending an interesting series of* *postcards on which some of the famous hawks of the Loo Hawking Club are depicted.*

Incidentally he remarks in his letter, in process of deploring the almost complete absence of falconers and trained hawks in France, owing to the hard times in France after the war, that he knows of one hawk only, a goshawk, belonging to M. Sourbets. 'The only trained goshawk I know of is one belonging to Sourbets. He had it from the eyrie in 1886. 34 years standing! It was still in good flying order when the war broke out.'

Gilbert Blaine finished the season on 7 October with 106 grouse in the bag.

The season of 1921 was interesting as the first season that Blaine tried seagull hawking on any scale. The grouse hawking still occupied most of their time and they started the season with eight peregrines, the two old intermewed passage falcons 'Lady Jane' and 'White Wings', a haggard falcon 'Dawn', and 'Ruth', a first season passage falcon, and four eyass falcons. The greatest disappointment to Blaine was the passage falcon 'Ruth', who, having shown great promise at mounting and waiting on, began sitting down when taken on to the moor. She coursed several grouse but had no chance and by the end of the week was refusing grouse put up right in front of her.

'Dawn', the haggard falcon, entered to grouse well. Put up on 20 August, she waited on quite well and caught a strong grouse that put into the road ditch after a long course. She was pulled out of a puddle, quite wet, with the grouse in her foot. Indeed 'Dawn' killed twelve grouse in good style, but on 26 August she took on a large gull, after waiting on patiently for grouse to be served her. She flew the gull keenly and went away right over Clyth, downwind, and was brought back to the lure. Flown again, she went hard at an old grouse, throwing up and stooping at him three times, and both disappeared over the bank near the road. She was picked up on a young common gull, which she was eating with relish when found.

To start with, Blaine tried flying 'Dawn' in a cast with one of the eyass falcons at gulls, but 'Dawn' did not like company at all and on 28 August, when she and one of the young Portland falcons were slipped together, 'Dawn' suddenly turned and caught the other hawk. On falling to the ground they separated, and then 'Dawn' went for the other hawk. Fighting like two game cocks, they fell into a stream together. Neither hawk appeared to be injured but when they were tied down near each other to dry 'Dawn' at once assumed a fighting attitude, tried to go for the young hawk and was evidently very angry. Afterwards, flown alone, she caught a young herring gull first stoop. This falcon became a gull hawk of the very finest and killed a total of thirty, a further three being caught with a companion. 'Dawn' flew in the very highest condition, getting hot blood every day except Sundays. She was fed chiefly upon the gulls she killed, eating both breasts and both legs of a herring gull at a meal, with half a grouse for a change.

Throughout that season the grouse hawking went well and they finished on 11 October with a brace to 'White Wings'. She went in her very best form and in her second flight put a grouse into the side of the loch, after flying across it. When flushed for her, he went to the road ditch, from which she drove him herself, and back he went again to the loch, crossing it again and putting in under the bank. Alec had him out of that

(opposite above) 'Anna Pavlova', a young Lundy falcon of 1912, sister to 'Barbara'

(opposite below) 'Barbara', an eyass peregrine falcon from Lundy. In her first season she accounted for 57 grouse

'Sylvia', an eyass peregrine falcon from Lundy in 1913. In her first season she accounted for 90 grouse and 2 partridge

(opposite above) Young falcon and tiercel, first season

(opposite below) Young falcon, first season

and he then went out into the loch, chased by 'White Wings', and dropped into the water. This manoeuvre was repeated by him again before the falcon caught him thigh deep in the water by the loch shore.

The score for the season was 170 grouse and eighty-one seagulls.

Blaine and Palmer were lucky in getting together an exceptionally good lot of hawks for the season of 1922. They started with ten peregrines, the two old stagers 'White Wings' and 'Lady Jane', 'Rhoda', a small passage falcon of 1921, 'Ariadne', a haggard falcon, and a good lot of eyasses including two from Lundy, the first obtained since 1914.

Captain Blaine's	'Lady Jane'	Passage Falcon	3 yrs old
Hawks	'Mary Rose'	Passage Falcon	2 yrs old
	'Rhoda'	Passage Falcon	1 yr old
	'Ariadne'	Haggard	
	'June'	Eyass Falcon	Young
Captain Palmer's	'White Wings'	Passage Falcon	3yrs old
Hawks	'Christmas'	Eyass Falcon	1 yr old
	Devon Falcon	Eyass Falcon	Young
	Dover Falcon	Eyass Falcon	Young
	'Lundy'	Eyass Tiercel	Young

The falcon and tiercel from Lundy were put out to hack on 5 June and were taken up after nearly six weeks. As usual, they showed great promise. The falcon named 'June' killed her first grouse, inadvertently put up by Alec, on 10 August, and another the following day. The tiercel killed a pigeon from a good pitch, in first rate style, on the second day on which he was flown loose.

'Lundy III', a Lundy tiercel of 1907

As so often happens, the 'Glorious Twelfth' opened with a strong S.E. wind and rain. However, the two Lundy eyasses each killed a grouse out of a covey marked down by the side of the road. 'Rhoda' and the Dover eyass each killed a squeaker. During the first few days of the season the hawks did not go at all well and straggled all over the moor. Indeed they weren't the only wanderers, for on the 14th Pilot, one of the setters, cleared half the moor before he could be taken up.

But soon the stars began to show their form and on the 16th: 'June' *killed a brace of grouse with ease.* 'Lundy' *went up beautifully and waited on, cut over an old cock, which got up again and he flew down into rushes. He then went up again and trussed it, when put out for him, like an old hawk.* 'Rhoda' *went on the soar, but coming over was luckily served well and trussed a grouse neatly out of a covey.* But not all were potential stars and the haggard 'Ariadne' put up two very bad performances and was lucky to kill two grouse. *Unless she improves she will not make a game hawk.*

2901.C.R.

By 24 August the team for the season had been sorted out and were filling the bag.

'June' *killed a brace with ease.*

'Lundy' *went high, waited on well and killed a brace.*

'Rhoda' *was again unlucky and could not be served. Flown again, after a very long 'wait on', during which Sybil pointed a hare and then a lark, she killed a grouse, trussing it without an effort. Both times she waited on most perseveringly and very high.*

'Lady Jane', *going magnificently, killed a single grouse from a fine pitch.*

'Ariadne' *sat down repeatedly and is quite hopeless as a grouse hawk.*

Little wind and midges very bad. Grouse very scarce towards Thrumster, and dogs not working well.

26 August: *E side of road beyond Badlibster. Wind variable from W to E and N. The Dover falcon killed a brace, not at all handsomely.*

'Rhoda' *went really well and killed a brace.*

'White Wings' *soared quite high and killed a grouse.*

'Lady Jane' *flew brilliantly and killed three grouse.*

Dogs again bad today, especially Sybil, who frequently set larks. Six brace of grouse killed. A good performance for the hawks, in spite of their not being quite in form today.

Two days later 'June' killed three grouse, her first flight a single grouse, from a vast pitch after soaring. In her second a covey rose to Free's point, and as 'June' was stooping a laggard got up. She changed to this, and cut it over dead right under Free's nose. The old bitch crept onto the grouse, and 'June' then caught her with both feet across her head. Free bore this with composure. Blaine released her from the hawk's grip, when 'June' immediately bound to Free's quarters. The falcon then jumped to the dead grouse. Free did not appear to hold it against the falcon, and later found a further grouse for her, which she caught after a long chase down to the burn.

7 September: 'Lundy' *killed three grouse. His second flight was most spectacular, as he cut over a single grouse rising to 'Sybil's' point from a high pitch right overhead, in full view of all the spectators, the grouse rebounding and rolling about 10 yards along the ground, apparently struck stone dead.*

The following day 'Lady Jane', *after killing one grouse, went away after a bevy of rooks over the Shepherd's House. The rooks began to ring, and she after them. One as*

Cadge of peregrines with dogs ready for the moor

An intermewed falcon

usual dropped out and she stooped at it down into the Camster Burn valley, where, however, she was unable to catch it. This rook then began to ring in earnest, 'Lady Jane', with no intention of being defeated, following him up. The rook held his own until they were very high, when the falcon got over him and brought him down a hundred feet or so. The rook gallantly began to ring again, and refused to be put down although 'Lady Jane' was over him and tried several times to cut in and force him to drop. She then gave up these tactics and began ringing above him harder than ever. The rook, seeing that he could no longer carry on upwards, made a long slanting dive with closed wings, appearing to aim for the corner of Camster plantation. 'Lady Jane' made a tremendous drive at him, threw up once, and then stooped again and disappeared with the rook below the horizon. Gough found her on the rook across the Camster Burn and about half a mile short of the plantation. This was a wonderful impromptu rook flight, worthy of the best of the Old Hawking Club.

13 September: *Six brace of grouse. 'White Wings' killed a brace, cutting over her second bird stone dead a few yards in front of Ken Palmer and Gough, in a cloud of feathers.*

The following letter was published in **The Field:**

Grouse Hawking in Caithness

You asked me to send you an account of our grouse hawking here, and I am taking the opportunity of a bad spell of weather to write. We were lucky in getting together a good lot of hawks. 223 grouse were scored up to 18 September, and a few various including seven gulls, and a blue hare weighing 3½ lbs, actually killed by 'June', the Lundy falcon. This hawk has the remarkable record of 56 grouse to her credit without a single miss. She is, I think, the fastest and most adroit 'footer' of any falcon I have ever seen. She does not go very high, but is very steady, and always catches grouse without assistance, even in the most awkward places.

The Lundy tiercel, her brother, is a most wonderful tiercel, and can kill grouse as well as a good falcon. He is a small tiercel with small feet, but the finest flyer I have ever seen. He goes to an immensely high 'pitch', and is as nippy as a sparrowhawk in catching grouse. He is also very fast, but lately has given us many anxious moments, having, like so many successful tiercels, become very unruly and difficult to manage. On 19 September he was twice very nearly lost, being almost out of sight in the sky and

An English setter on the moor

refusing to come down, and TOO HIGH to get up to grouse before they could 'put in'. He also was joined by a young wild falcon, and completely held his own with her in flying, and the other day he played with a wild tiercel, being the aggressor all the time, and having the command in flying. He is the only trained hawk I have ever seen whose pace and style is indistinguishable from that of a wild one. He has killed 48 grouse up to 20 September. The young passage falcon 'Rhoda' is also a very promising one, and a very pretty flyer.

We had hopes of killing 200 brace with the hawks this year, but I am afraid the weather is against us, for we have had two bad weeks without being able to get out for several days.

G. Blaine.

Camster Lodge, Caithness.

Despite the weather, the hawks continued to kill grouse in style. On the 21st 'Lundy' went remarkably, after being kept in for two days and fed on rabbit. He as usual mounted to a great pitch in spite of the wind and killed two grouse in perfect form. The following day he was lost for three hours and finally found by Mackay, the keeper, and was taken up with a bulging crop.

9 October: *'June' killed three, including her 80th grouse without a miss. 'Lundy' went brilliantly and killed three. 'Rhoda' a brace. This hawk is getting very good. 'White Wings' killed a brace. 'Lady Jane' killed three. To kill thirteen grouse with five hawks on 9 October is no mean achievement.*

Despite Blaine's doubts in his letter to **The Field**, the total bag crept nearer and nearer to two hundred brace and finally, on 23 October,

111

'White Wings' had the honour of killing the four-hundredth grouse, the others bringing the total to 405. Although 1922 must be recorded in the annals of the sport, it has to be remembered that the score of 406 grouse taken in 1913 must stand as the record, and that score was achieved in a season shorter by a week.

	Total grouse	Various	Total killed	Unsuccessful Flights	Not served with quarry	Number of flights	Average	Weights of hawks at end of season
'Lady Jane'	75	3	78	6	1	85	92.8	2lbs 1oz
'White Wings'	72	—	72	12	—	84	85.5	2lbs 4oz
'June'	99	1	100	2	1	103	98	2lbs 2oz
'Rhoda'	57	1	58	10	6	74	85.3	2lbs 1oz
'Lundy'	75	1	76	5	—	81	93.8	1lb 6oz
'Ariadne'	7	8	15	14	1	30	51.7	2lbs 2oz
Dover Falcon	20	1	21	14	2	37	60	
'Christmas'	—	1	1	5	—	6	—	
	405	16	421					

Daily average of grouse: 7.5
No of days flown: 54

Summary: *A very strong team of game hawks took the field this year, rivalling perhaps that of 1913, which was 'Sylvia's' year. The falcon and tiercel from Lundy well upheld the reputation of their race.*

The tiercel was a hawk of surpassing excellence, and his score of 75 grouse, maintained right into the middle of October, is probably the record for a tiercel. His pitch and style of stooping were very fine. His sister 'June' was a most successful and deadly falcon at grouse, but she would not mount to a really good pitch, no doubt relying on her speed and cleverness of catching, and so did not give the same pleasure as the other hawks to the spectators.

'Rhoda', a very charming little passage falcon, made her debut this season, and by the end of it was everything that a good grouse hawk should be. She had a fine dashing style of getting up to her pitch, when she would wait on perfectly, and not too slavishly, and had a clever way of footing grouse, stooping up to one side of them and then making a sudden drive into them from a flank. This manoeuvre was nearly always successful, and this falcon trussed more grouse than any other hawk.

The old ones, 'Lady Jane' and 'White Wings', flew consistently well throughout the season, and the latter went better than she has ever been before. Her stoops and the drive at the end of them were harder than those of any other hawk. This falcon, a very large one, always takes a long time to get really fit, and appears to fly better in colder weather. 'Lady Jane' went in her usual finished style. For the rest there is little to relate.

In 1923 there was no grouse hawking. In consequence of the exceptional spell of bad weather from May and onwards till the middle of July, the stock of grouse had almost been wiped out. The alternative was to fly the young hawks at gulls of which they killed forty-nine.

By 1924 the grouse situation had improved a little but even so Palmer

Thomas Mann's Rook Hawking Party from an oil painting by G. E. Lodge in 1889. Mann stands near the Hawk cadge, holding a peregrine falcon and dressed in the green coat of the Old Hawking Club.

His professional falconer, Alfred Frost, is kneeling by the cadge and is setting down another falcon.

Behind this falcon sits 'Vic', a passage peregrine, and at the other end of the cadge is a saker falcon, the property of Captain C. W. Thomson, thought to be the mounted gentleman to the left of the picture.

Beside Mann stands Mr Taylor, a regular sporting companion of Mann. Seated beyond Mr Taylor, is the artist, George Lodge.

Richard Best with two of Blaine's setters

and Blaine started hawking a week later than usual. Two new passage hawks that had been flown on the Plain at rooks in the spring, 'Nydia' and 'Yellowfoot', were tried but found to be wanting and the only new hawk made was another Lundy tiercel belonging to Captain Palmer.

In thirty days flying the five hawks flown scored 131 grouse and Gilbert Blaine noted at the end of the season: *We have done much better than we had expected with the hawks this season. At first grouse appeared to be as scarce as last year but as the season advanced more and more came in, until in October hawks were able to be flown quite quickly without covering much ground. The birds killed were generally in good condition and it appears as though the grouse disease has been stamped out. The new tiercel, 'Lundy II', has proved a first-class little game hawk. He is not such an attractive flyer as old 'Lundy', but faster and very deadly. He has*

(opposite) 'White Wings', a passage peregrine falcon, 1920-24. The property of Ken Palmer, she accounted for 176 grouse

Tiercel moulting into blue plumage.

'Greenfoot', a peregrine tiercel from a
gouache by G. E. Lodge.

(*opposite*) Peregrine tiercel on a partridge, oil
painting by G. E. Lodge on a door panel.

A jerkin eyass. Taken in Iceland by Ernest Vesey in 1936, it was flown at grouse by Gilbert Blaine

also become very steady. '*Lady Jane*' *has been very steady all this season, and* '*Rhoda*' *going better all the time.* '*White Wings*' *also is just getting into her October form again.*

Although a big bag of grouse has not been made, sport has been of a high class. It has been a hard season for the dogs, owing to the amount of running they often had to do before getting a point. The work has tried them very highly, and has not done them any good.

Again in 1925, Blaine and Palmer relied on a very promising entry of wild-caught hawks, including a haggard falcon and a red tiercel. Of these 'Lancia' and 'Primrose', a Club falcon, had flown with success at rooks in the spring, while the haggard, 'Flying Duchess', had shown great promise, but had contracted a bad attack of 'croaks' and had to be put aside, after killing a few rooks. 'White Wings' had unfortunately died in the summer at Hawley, so Captain Palmer's hawks were all tiercels. Grouse again appeared to be none too plentiful. However, in thirty-nine hawking days the hawks put together the very creditable score of 132 grouse and 'Lundy II' very nearly added a woodcock to the bag.

19 October: *When he got up again to a fair height having put in a snipe, a woodcock was flushed upwind, and the tiercel, from a long way back, went in pursuit. He made a slanting stoop up to it, which it evaded, then threw up and stooped again. The woodcock again jumped and then went in a long circle with the tiercel hot on its tail. The woodcock, unable to shake him off, and obviously bent on putting in at first, then went straight on downwind, rising obliquely all the time, the tiercel still pursuing. They went up and up and away, the woodcock slightly above and to the right of the hawk, until they went clean out of sight of my glasses and Mackay's telescope, in a direction between the Wick burn and Badlibster. When last seen both were still going hard some yards apart, and both on the same level. 'Young Lundy' was not found and had to be left out.*

An eyass falcon on her kill in the heather

9

Viscount Portal
of Hungerford

The saying 'Once a falconer, always a falconer' has, in these pages, been shown to be true of many of those who have followed the sport. Certainly it seems to be true of those that have pursued the sport with real enthusiasm and success. However, one highly successful falconer, although no doubt thinking often of falconry, actually practised the sport for only a few short but exciting seasons, Viscount Portal of Hungerford, Marshal of the Royal Air Force, first became interested in falconry while still a pupil at Winchester. Returning home across the Berkshire Downs with his father in September, 1907, they saw a party out hawking partridges, complete with a cadge full of peregrines, dogs and falconers. Stopping, young Charles Portal met Captain Gilbert Blaine and so, from the very start, had for example and teaching the very best falconer of that time. On the cadge that year was an immature eyass tiercel, 'Lundy III', who for eight seasons was to serve Blaine as a game hawk equal to any trained by falconers through the ages. In the season of 1907 this tiercel killed fifty-eight partridges. Inspired by watching such outstanding hawks, Charles Portal soon acquired a hawk of his own, though only fourteen years old. It was a jack merlin, given him by Gilbert Blaine. Other hawks followed, more merlins, sparrowhawks, goshawks and peregrines, some kept at school, others while at Oxford.

The four years of the First World War made hawking impossible, but in 1919 Charles Portal was sent to R.A.F. Cranwell, in Lincolnshire. The aerodrome at Cranwell was well stocked with partridges and covered more than three thousand acres, highly suited to game hawking, and multitudes of larks showed promise for flights with merlins. Not surprisingly, Charles Portal started the season of 1920 with a cast of Yorkshire merlins and an eyass peregrine tiercel, obtained from Gilbert Blaine, who also hacked him. The merlins took a total of 105 skylarks and the tiercel killed twenty-three partridges before being lost on 17 September. To replace him Blaine again came to Portal's help with an eyass falcon of the year that was not quite high enough in her mounting to take grouse throughout the season. Portal entered her to partridges and she killed a further twenty-three before being lost at the end of January.

Still stationed at Cranwell, Charles Portal started the season of 1921 in a much bigger way. A falconer, George Blake, had been trained for him

(*opposite*) 'Lundy II', a peregrine tiercel, from an oil painting by G. E. Lodge.
A fine eyass tiercel of 1924, the property of Captain Kenneth Palmer.

Charles Portal in 1922, partridge hawking near Tilshead on Salisbury Plain

121

Stanley Allen lark hawking

An eyass tiercel, the property of Charles Portal

by Best at Shrewton, during the spring rook hawking of the Old Hawking Club. Four merlins, again from Yorkshire, were hard penned in a dry loft, and, trained quickly, they were in the field by 17 July. The three 'jacks' became increasingly cunning as, at this early date, the young larks were extremely easy to catch and the 'jacks' quickly learnt to leave any difficult birds in expectation of easier chances. However, the female 'June' turned out to be an outstandingly successful lark hawk, never refusing, and took 162 larks between 17 July and the beginning of September, in forty-three flying days. The total of larks taken by the merlins was 186.

Three peregrine tiercels were hacked and Portal kept the two most likely to make game hawks and named them 'Pirate' and 'Rattle'. 'Pirate' killed a total of forty-one partridges and three various, being particularly clever at catching partridge as they slowed to put in to cover, but, not being much of a mounter, he did not show much sport. His brother, 'Rattle', was a hawk of outstanding excellence and, once entered, he became, in Charles Portal's estimation, the very best tiercel he ever saw fly. An independent hawk, he would not come freely to the lure but would remain, waiting on, for a partridge to be flushed under him, when he generally killed it. He was flown on eighty-four days, ending in January, and took a total of 121 partridges and a handful of various.

The following season found Charles Portal at the Staff College at Andover; plenty of work to do but oh so near to the open downland of Salisbury Plain. There Portal shared the game rights on land near Shrewton, Tilshead and Orcheston, amounting to more than three thousand acres, with Major Stanley Allen, the rent being one shilling an acre. Once again they started with the merlins of which they hacked nine at Shrewton and kept three, a jack and two females. The merlins were out for a maximum of twenty-eight days and took a total of 286 skylarks in

370 flights. The lark hawking was rather spoilt by the bad weather and the weakness of many of the larks, even on the open down. The merlins' scores were as follows:

Name	Flights	Kills	Killed in Air	Ringers Killed	Percentage of Kills to Flights
'Angeline'	133	100	20	11	75%
'Squeak'	158	134	42	16	85%
'Wilfred'	79	52	6	4	65%
Total	370	286	68	31	

'Squeak' was a very fine flyer, and became very deadly towards the end of August. She killed over forty skylarks without a miss and often bettered wild merlins that joined in the flights. 'Squeak' was once attacked by a wild female hobby after she had taken a lark in a good flight. The hobby snatched the lark from 'Squeak' and made off with it, but the merlin went hard after the hobby and with her second stoop forced the hobby to drop the lark, which then flew away, seemingly unhurt.

'Angeline' also enjoyed the occasional bout with a wild hawk. In one flight she had just fetched her ringing lark when she was joined by a wild female merlin who promptly footed the lark. 'Angeline' then stooped at the wild merlin, forcing it to drop the lark in the air. The lark made off as hard as it could but was caught again by the wild merlin. 'Angeline', not to be outdone, made another stoop at the wild one and snatched the lark from her, then proceeded to chase the wild one off the ground, all the while carrying her prey.

The jack, 'Wilfred', was not in the same class as the other two but was extraordinarily skilful at taking larks when they put in to cover. He would crash into nettles or thorn bushes and invariably came out with a lark in his foot.

With the partridges they had excellent sport. There were a few backward coveys which caused some trouble in September, the hawks carrying them, but on the whole the partridges were strong and plentiful. They started the season with five peregrines — the intermewed tiercel 'Rattle', three eyass tiercels from Horn Head and an eyass falcon from a Devon eyrie. This falcon was taken much too young and arrived in the down. For a fortnight she took all her meal from the hand and then was put out to hack for five weeks. While at hack she showed little style and became a confirmed screamer. On being taken up from hack, she developed 'croaks' badly, but once on the wing she quickly improved and, once entered to quarry, she gave up screaming. She not only flew magnificently, but from the very beginning seemed to know what was expected of her. She became a high mounter, fast, tractable and as deadly at stooping and footing as any hawk could be. Her strongest point was her understanding of where to position herself when the birds were flushed and how to deal with them in difficult places. She was always willing and seemed to mount higher and stoop harder as the day went on. Between 23 September and 23 October, she killed fifty-one partridges without a miss, a feat which few shots could claim to achieve.

Of the tiercels, 'Rattle' was unfortunately lost when he soared away

Stanley Allen with his jack merlin, 'Joey'

while being flown to the lure; 'Orion', one of Major Allen's tiercels, was also lost after killing three partridges early in the season. 'Sirius', Major Allen's other tiercel, was a very high mounter and stooped beautifully, but was not so clever with his feet. Consequently his stylish stooping sometimes failed to add anything to the bag, for downland partridges, in October and November, can shift with the greatest of ease from the rake of a badly aimed stoop. The last of the three brothers, the tiercel 'Mike', was very fast and a clever footer, but would not mount well and was not so rewarding to see fly. Their successes were as follows:

Name	Flights	Partridges	Various	Total
'Sibella'	177	161	4	165
'Mike'	130	111	—	111
'Sirius'	94	65	5	70
'Orion'	3	3	—	3
Total	404	340	9	349

The best day of the season produced a bag of twelve partridges and a pheasant in thirteen flights, and in October too. The party usually consisted of four or five people, with two spaniels, and an old setter, but often Portal would be out with just George Blake and the dogs. As one would expect with so many days spent out on the downs, different happenings made interest of every day. On one occasion a hard-pressed partridge dashed into a pond and swam round for some time with only its head and neck showing out of the water. Another partridge tried to hide under a cow who obviously didn't approve, for she kicked the partridge out to the waiting hawk. Some partridges were killed by flying into barbed-wire fences; one broke its neck when it flew into a tree. But as well as these incidentals many days were remembered by the brilliant flights of the hawks, days when 'Sibella' would stoop and cut over one bird from a covey and take a second, binding to it after a stoop from her throw-up.

That glorious season was the last that Lord Portal enjoyed with hawks of his own. His was a short life as a practical falconer but with such successes Charles Portal joins well with those others that are 'Celebrated Falconers of the Past'.

A peregrine tiercel

(*opposite*) Reeks, falconer with 'Mintha', a peregrine; Stanley Allen with 'Tarina', a peregrine, and the ladies with a sparrow-hawk.

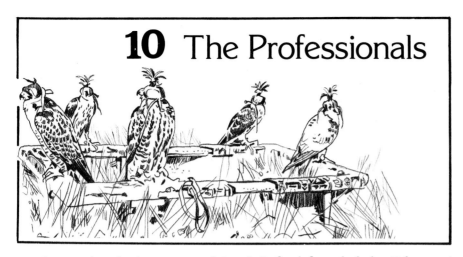

10 The Professionals

When Colonel Thornton and Lord Orford founded the Falconers' Club in about 1770 sport was still to be had at kite and heron. For this they used passage falcons caught at Valkenswaard in Holland and the professional falconers were nearly all Dutchmen. Versed in the management and training of passage hawks, and of flying quarry from the hood, in contrast to waiting on flights at game, the Dutch falconers brought their skills to England.

One such falconer, Jan Daams, came to England when about twenty-eight years old, as falconer to Lord Orford. When Lord Orford died, Daams stayed with the Falconers' Club under Colonel Wilson in Norfolk. Every autumn Daams travelled to Valkenswaard to obtain fresh-taken passage hawks for the English Club but in 1808 he was arrested under orders from Louis Bonaparte. Daams (sometimes spelt Daims) was ordered to set up a mews at Het Loo near Apeldoorn, and there he stayed until Louis Bonaparte abdicated in 1810. Daams was then put in charge of the hawking establishment at Versailles by Napoleon and eventually returned to Valkenswaard where he died in 1829.

Frank van der Heuvell, another native of Valkenswaard, joined Colonel Thornton in 1794. Falconer to Thornton for five years, he then worked for Lord Middleton and Sir Rober Lawley until 1820 when he was engaged by Colonel Wilson for a further eight seasons. The three brothers, Arnold, James and Jan Bots, all worked at one time or another at Didlington for Colonel Wilson (later Lord Berners) and all later returned to Valkenswaard as falconers to the Loo Club. Jan, while working for the Loo Club, made an expedition to Norway to catch gyrfalcons. He was most successful, taking nine or ten, all passage falcons. Of these it appears that only two were successful at quarry.

Another family from Valkenswaard who came to England were the Peels or Pells. Father John Pells first worked for Sir John Sebright with whom he enjoyed good sport at partridge, magpie and crow until 1814. Pells then went to Didlington to work for Colonel Wilson. As with other falconers, Pells travelled each year to Holland to trap fresh passage hawks and then to train them for heron hawking. About 1827 Pells made a permanent home in England where he died in 1838. His two sons were both born in England. The younger son, Henry, worked as a falconer to

(opposite) John Pells

Peter Ballantyne with his grandson, Willie

Valkenswaard, Holland. The hawk trapper's equipment

Mr O'Keefe in Ireland; the older son, John, was assistant to his father at Didlington. On leaving Colonel Wilson's employment, father and son looked after the hawks of the Duke of Leeds and the Earl of Aberdeen and later became falconers to the Hereditary Grand Falconer of England, the Duke of St Albans. In 1842 he joined the falconers to the Loo Club and it was Pells who brought over the two famous heron hawks, 'Sultan' and 'De Ruyter', to Newcome in Norfolk. The Duke of Leeds, an enthusiastic member of the Loo Club, sent Pells to Iceland in 1845. With all the skill of the Dutch hawk trappers, he succeeded in trapping fifteen gyrfalcons. The Duke of Leeds kept seven of these lovely falcons, some of which were trained for hare hawking; the other eight he gave to the Loo Hawking Club and they were entered to heron but only one or two turned out well.

After living for some time at Mr Newcome's estate at Feltwell, Pells retired to Lakenheath on a pension from the Duke of St Albans and there continued to train a few falcons but, surrounded by partridge manors, had little chance of hawking. Major Charles Hawkins Fisher, who spent much time with Pells after meeting him by chance in 1858, found him a silent, morose man who thawed now and then under the influence of his favourite gin and his pipe, which he was seldom without. Pells had a poor opinion of gentlemen falconers, with the exception of Edward Clough Newcome, but helped many falconers with his knowledge and skills.

The Mollen family were perhaps the best known and probably the best remembered of the Valkenswaard falconers and hawk trappers. Adrian Mollen was trained by Jan Bots whilst serving as assistant to him in the employ of Lord Berners at Didlington. There until 1836, Mollen then removed to Austria to work for Prince Trautmansdorff, where the principal sport was game hawking. While there he trained saker falcons, possibly a Dutch falconer's first experience of a desert falcon. He returned to Holland in 1841, becoming one of two Head Falconers to the Loo Club and in 1850 became Head Falconer to the King of Holland. After the closure of the heron hawking at Het Loo, Mollen, aided by his sons, continued to trap passage falcons for European falconers and the Old Hawking Club of England in particular. The Mollens also made the Dutch hawk hoods for which they became so well known, and other equipment required by falconers. This Karl Mollen continued to do after

Valkenswaard, Holland. The trapper waiting for action

<table>
<tr>
<td>

Prix-Courant
DES
FOURNITURES DE
FAUCONNERIE,

de **CHARLES TH. MOLLEN**,
à **Valkenswaard**, (Hollande).

On est prié d'envoyer le montant d'avance et l'expédition des fournitures aura lieu immédiatement après.

Poche de Chasse . .	== fr. 25.—.
Chaperon	,, 2.40.
Chaperon de rust .	,, 1.20.
Grelot indien	,, 2.40.
Grelot commun . . .	,, 1.50.
Vervelle	,, 1.20.
Longe	,, 0.60.
Jettes	,, 0.40.
Leurre	,, 6.00.
Frais de transport .	,, ...

</td>
<td>

Price List of Articles
WANTED FOR
FALCONRY,

from **CHARLES TH. MOLLEN**,
at **Valkenswaard**, (Holland).

Please remit money and furnitures will immediately be forwarded.

Falconersbag . . . pd. st.	1 - 0 - 0
Hood	0—2—0.
Rufter hood	0—1—0.
Indianbell	0—2—0.
Commonbell	0-1-3.
Swivel	0-1-0.
Leash	0-0-6.
Jesses	0-0-4.
Lure	0—5—0.
Postcarriage	10

</td>
</tr>
<tr>
<td>

Prix-Courant
DES
OISEAUX DE CHASSE
NON DRESSÉS,

Faucon rouge	== fr.
Tiercelet	,, -
Hagard	,, -
Autour	,, -
Emérillon	,, -
Epervier	,, -

VOTRE DÉVOUÉ SERVITEUR,
Ch. Th. Mollen.

VALKENSWAARD, date de la poste.

</td>
<td>

Price List of Wild
CAUGHT BIRDS.

Red falcon	pd. st.	3 - 10 -
Red tiercel	,, ,,	3 - -
Haggerd falcon	,, ,,	3 . . . .
Goshawk . . *are no more on the passage*
Merlin	,, ,,	1
Sparrowhawk	,, ,,	1

YOURS RESPECTFULLY
Ch. Th. Mollen.

VALKENSWAARD, date postmark.

for taming a bird I only charge three shillings each

</td>
</tr>
</table>

Karl Mollen's price list

129

Valkenswaard, Holland. A peregrine in the bow net

the death of his father, until his last order in 1930. Keeping careful note of orders, Karl Mollen's old books are an important record of the falconers of that time. He made over one thousand hawk hoods, also falconers' bags of green baize, swivels, bells, jesses and leashes, but no hawking gloves. The annual order of eight or so red falcons from the Old Hawking Club soon became the mainstay of the business and on the closing down of the Club in 1926 Mollen gave up trapping and the tradition so long associated with Valkenswaard came to an end.

Although the profession of falconer was dominated to a large extent by the Dutch, it must not be thought that all falconers in Britain in the early nineteenth century were Dutch. Certainly many gentlemen falconers who kept eyasses for game hawking preferred the Scottish falconers, such as Tom Kennedy, falconer to Lord O'Neil, Francis M'Cullock, falconer to Colonel Bonham, and the famous John Anderson, falconer to Mr Malcolm Fleming of Barochan in Renfrewshire. John Anderson was born in 1745, at Currie, near Edinburgh, and as soon as he was old enough was employed as assistant falconer to John Hainshaw at Barochan Tower. When Hainshaw retired, Anderson became head falconer to Mr Fleming, who at that time kept the Renfrewshire Subscription Hawks. There the hawks were mainly flown at partridge and woodcock. In about 1818 Peter Ballantyne, who was to become equally as famous as Anderson, joined him at Barochan as assistant falconer. On the death of Mr Fleming in 1819, both Anderson and Ballantyne continued at Barochan in charge of the Renfrewshire Subscription Hawks. Anderson retired in 1832 and died the following year.

Peter Ballantyne (or Ballantine) was born in 1798, at Dumfries House, Ayrshire, and acquired his love of hawks and hawking from his father, who at one time had been falconer to the Earl of Eglinton, and from his father's close friend, John Anderson. When Anderson retired, Ballantyne took service with Lord Carmarthen, later to become the Duke of Leeds, as assistant to John Pells senior. Lord Carmarthen's hawks were kept at Huntly Lodge, Aberdeenshire, and while Pells trained passage hawks, using the Dutch methods, Ballantyne trained eyass peregrines. Here he had the opportunity to combine the best of the schools of falconry and by this was to become a falconer versed in all types of hawking and

successful beyond average at game hawking. Leaving Lord Carmarthen, he worked for a while for Sir James Boswell of Auchinleck. Here he also managed a successful greyhound kennels, as well as training some falcons each season. After twenty-five years at Auchinleck, Ballantyne moved to Ewenfield in Ayrshire. There he worked for Mr Robert Ewen and their successes at game hawking clearly show Ballantyne's skill in the art of falconry. Most of the sport was at partridge and two of the best tiercels flown during this period were 'The Imp' and 'Rantin' Robin'. 'Rantin' Robin' was flown for ten seasons and was from an inland cliff that Ballantyne considered produced eyasses of the highest class. With hawks such as these high scores were sure. In 1870 269 head of quarry were taken, in 1871 346 and in 1873 367.

John Barr

The 1870 team consisted of:

'Ginglin' Geordie' young tiercel	46 head
'Jan Van' young falcon	54 head
'Band of Hope' six-year tiercel	49 head
'Rantin' Robin' five-year tiercel	47 head
'The Imp' three-year tiercel	54 head
'Moss Rose' falcon	19 head

	269

On the death of Mr Ewen, who, as well as having been a keen falconer, was for many years master of the Ayrshire Harriers, Ballantyne moved to Auchincruive, and there, as falconer to Mr R. A. Oswald, continued to show fine sport, one falcon named 'Pearl' being of particular excellence. At the age of eighty-six, still with a hawk in training, Peter Ballantyne died at Auchincruive.

Another family of Scottish falconers were the Barrs. William Barr the elder was gamekeeper and falconer to Sir John Maxwell of Pollack, who was an active member of the Renfrewshire Subscription Hawks, and no doubt William Barr knew both Anderson and Peter Ballantyne. All three sons were capable men with a hawk, but it is his two sons, Robert and John, who are best remembered. The eldest brother William was a clever hand with hawks but emigrated to Australia in 1853.

John Barr, the second son, was probably the first of the professionals successfully to combine all the different methods used in falconry.

131

Valkenswaard, Holland. Back to the hide

Robert Barr

Trained in Scotland, he became a first-class falconer in the management of eyass hawks. From 1857 to 1865, as falconer to His Highness The Maharajah Dhuleep Singh, he travelled through Syria and Southern Europe and mixed with the falconers of the Middle East. He journeyed yearly to Holland to help trap and train the annual requirement of passage peregrines. Gerald Lascelles wrote of John Barr that he was probably the cleverest falconer of the nineteenth century. A real lover of hawks, he thoroughly fathomed the mysteries of catching, taming and training a hawk. There was no quarry that he had not flown at, no kind of hawking that was not familiar to him. Together with his nephew, Jamie Barr, son of his elder brother William, who was later to become falconer to Major Charles Hawkins Fisher, John visited Iceland in 1869 and there successfully caught thirty gyrfalcons for the Champagne Hawking Club. These gyrs were trained at Elvedon Hall, near Thetford, then the home of Maharajah Dhuleep Singh where all the hawks belonging to the Champagne Club had been removed when war broke out between France and Germany in 1870.

On the death of Mr Clough Newcome the Old Hawking Club had broken up. Robert Barr, John's younger brother, had taken employment with the Marquess of Bute and the Club hawks were divided up between the members. In 1870 Lascelles and Robert Barr spent Easter on the Plain, rook hawking, and in the autumn of 1871, Gerald Lascelles, A. E. Knox and Cecil Duncombe met at Gordon Castle, as guests of the Duke of Richmond. There they agreed to restart the Old Hawking Club. Old Club members were contacted and Lord Lilford, in particular, gave generously. Gerald Lascelles became manager and secretary to the Club and remained in office until 1914.

Robert Barr having died, John Barr was employed and a start was made in the spring of 1872. A first-class team of passage hawks was got together and flown at Ashdown on the Berkshire Downs, Lord Craven being an enthusiastic supporter of the Old Hawking Club, and for some of the season on the Plain in Wiltshire.

Again the following season John Barr showed excellent sport and even succeeded in taking a few wild peewits with a cast of two passage tiercels,

'The Earl' and 'The Doctor'. Thought to be almost uncatchable with a trained hawk, the peewits has long been tried by falconers in the vain hope of success. At the same time as Barr was making the attempt to take peewits he daily exercised his hawks on the Curragh in Ireland where he was at that time. There, much to Barr's delight, a scruffy-looking wild tiercel, who still had one jess on to show that he too had at one time been a falconer's bird, daily caught one of the many wild peewits frequenting the Curragh with relative ease.

John Barr only stayed with the Old Hawking Club for two short seasons, then, employed by Captain Dugmore, he spent a further two seasons as falconer to the New Falconry Club. Started on an ambitious scale the new club employed four falconers. Hawks were flown in Ireland and England, and displays given in the gardens of the Jardin d'Acclimatisation in Paris and at Alexandra Palace in London. During his time with Captain Dugmore, John Barr again showed his expertise at catching hawks. During the summer of 1876 he went to Norway to catch gyrfalcons for the New Falconry Club and returned two months later with ten gyrs and as many goshawks as he could manage.

With the closing down of the New Falconry Club, John Barr became falconer to Mr T. Evans of Sawston in Cambridgeshire where he trained several good rook hawks in that spring but died later that same year at the early age of thirty-nine.

John Barr's younger brother served his apprenticeship with his elder brother and for a time was in the employment of Prince Dhuleep Singh. Later he became falconer to the Old Hawking Club in its early days when it developed from the spring rook hawking on Salisbury Plain started by Cecil Duncombe and Major Fisher in 1863.

The following year a small club was formed under the able management of Edward Clough Newcome. The premier sport was the spring rook hawking on the Plain with the odd flight at heron in Norfolk. Club members also enjoyed grouse hawking on moors taken in Perthshire. For seven seasons Robert Barr, helped by the considerable skills and knowledge of Mr Newcome, showed sport of the highest class, but just before the death of Newcome the Club was disbanded and Robert Barr became falconer to the Marquess of Bute. In his service he died in September, 1870, at Cardiff Castle.

While Robert Barr was in the employ of the Old Hawking Club in its early days, under the management of Edward Clough Newcome, the hawks were kept at that gentleman's home at Feltwell Hall, Hockwold in Norfolk. The head keeper at Feltwell then was M. Frost, and his son John was brought up among hawks, immediately showing an aptitude for working with them. John learnt much from Mr Newcome, always so willing to pass on his knowledge and skills to others, and of course from Robert Barr. Indeed for a while John was employed as under-falconer to Barr. Nearby lived Pells, the last of the Dutch falconers still in England, and no doubt young Frost journeyed to Lakenheath to talk to Pells and to learn what he could from him. Lascelles, when reforming the Old Hawking Club, took on young John Frost as assistant to John Barr, and on Barr leaving the Club in 1873, Frost became Head Falconer and was with the Old Hawking Club until his death in 1890.

John Frost, son of Michael Frost and falconer to the Old Hawking Club

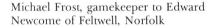

Michael Frost, gamekeeper to Edward Newcome of Feltwell, Norfolk

To start with the headquarters of the club were at Oakhurst, near Leeds, on the Harewood Estates, then the residence of the Hon Gerald Lascelles, but upon Lascelles' appointment as Deputy Surveyor of the New Forest in 1880, Club hawks, plus falconer and family, moved to Lyndhurst, Lascelles taking up residence in the Queen's House. John Frost, married and with three children, moved into a thatched cottage at Bank, which had a good garden and paddock. Frost was an all round sportsman; with hawk and gun he excelled; he also had a famous strain of working terriers, and some good game cocks. He was well able to take care of himself with his fists and could easily walk four miles in an hour. He loved a good horse and shortly after moving to Bank he bought a couple of Forest ponies for his children to ride. His eldest son soon became so expert that he was in constant demand as a jockey in local pony races. Despite his involvement in the pony racing, Frost never betted, deeming that a fool's game. The only sport he found no pleasure in was fishing which he considered too slow. When not busy with the Club hawks, the New Forest was a fine place to be, with otter hunting, badger digging, pigeon shooting and helping the Forest keepers with doe shooting when reducing their numbers in November.

At Lyndhurst the mews were in what had been the original stables before the new stabling was built on the opposite side of the road, and afforded a lot of interest to visitors to the Queen's House or the Verderer's Hall. Perhaps even more interesting to the villagers were the young hawks flying at hawk. As John Frost's son wrote in later years: *These hawks were obtained from various eyries around the coast, including one from Culvercliff in the Isle of Wight. Taken from the nest before they could fly they knew nothing about preying for themselves, having had their food laid before them by the parent birds, a task taken up by the falconer. The hack-board or feeding place was in a field in front of the Queen's House and these young hawks were flying in perfect liberty for a period of approximately three weeks every late spring. They made the Church their landmark and the pinnacles their roosting place, not without leaving their mark on the Church below. The Rev Coglan, then Curate-in-Charge, once jocularly remarked to the falconer, John Frost, 'You know you ought to get up there and wash that off?' to which he received the retort, 'Aye, I will if you will come up and hold the bucket for me.'*

As their powers of flight developed, the young hawks would roam the countryside for miles around, but as time for the evening meal drew near they would re-assemble and then there would follow such a show of aerobatics as no airman could hope to emulate, chasing each other around the Church, stooping, twisting and turning, all the while uttering their short scream from the fullness of their enjoyment.

At the termination of the hack they were caught and their initial training began. It was a source of interest to the villagers to meet the falconer and his assistant with their hooded hawks on their way to the racecourse for that purpose. Once one of the hawks, while at hack, got entangled on one of the pinnacles and would assuredly have remained there but for one brave spirit, a Jack Barnes, who, with other helpers, mounted the belfry, pushed a plank through a window, and with the others holding the inner end got out onto the plank and with a long stick released the hawk, a test of nerve beyond the average man. For this he

'Jack' Frost with Dr Arbel's falcons at Vadancourt

received the princely reward of £1, but that was in the good old days, when, as one worthy used to say, 'You could go into a pub on a Saturday night with a "tanner", get a pint of beer, an ounce of "baccy" and a clay pipe and come out with a ha'penny change.'

Every autumn Frost would travel to Holland, there to collect and start the training of the passage peregrines taken for the Old Hawking Club, and there, of course, Frost mixed with and learnt from the Dutch falconers. Rook hawking continued to be the major sport but Frost proved himself to be just as skilled in the game hawking field. Lascelles, writing of John Frost in the **Coursing and Falconry** volume of The Badminton Library, says: *With the exception of John Barr, Frost has had no rival as an all-round falconer during the present* [nineteenth] *century, and it is hard to say what perfection the sport, as adapted to modern times and methods, might not have attained under his intelligent care and unfailing keenness. As a first-rate sportsman he excelled, and with dog, gun, or hawk was equally good. With an education and an intelligence not commonly met with in persons of his station, he was not only an admirable servant, but an interesting companion, clever at all sports, and as such, and as a friend, he will be most regretted by all those who knew him best.*

Frost died when only thirty-six, while grouse hawking in September, 1890. Engaged for grouse hawking by the Duke of Portland, a member of

(opposite above) John (Jack) Frost, son of John Frost

(opposite below) George Oxer with a rook hawk on Salisbury Plain. He became Head Falconer to the Old Hawking Club after the death of John Frost

James Rutford, falconer to Major Fisher, with two young hawks at Riddlehamhope, 1897

the Old Hawking Club, Frost succeeded in taking ninety-six grouse with a team of four Club peregrines during the last few weeks of his life. He was buried at Berriedale in Caithness, where a memorial was erected by members of the Hawking Club. Undoubtedly he was one of the cleverest of falconers, for the scores of the Club hawks while under his care were consistent and excellent. In 1882 the hawks killed 100 brace of grouse between 12 August and 14 September. The total return for the year 1887 was 576 head, including 209 rooks. In 1890 the Club hawks took a total of 244 rooks. Such returns speak for themselves.

John Frost junior, second son of Old John, also became a falconer. Born in April, 1878, at Oakhurst, near Leeds, he never really knew life without hawks around him. For a while he was assistant falconer to George Oxer at the Old Hawking Club, but also worked abroad for a time as falconer to Dr Arbel of the Château de Vadancourt. While with Dr Arbel 'Jack' Frost flew hawks at the International Falconry Contest at Spa, in Belgium. Like his father, he was as clever a dog handler as he was a falconer and he looked after Captain Blaine's 'Westdown' kennels of English setters. Blaine, in reporting on his successes at grouse hawking in 1912, says of the dogs: *The three Setters used, Griff, Belle, and Glee, did wonderful service, and had it not been for the excellence of their work, the hawks would never have done so well. The hawks could always be served at the right moment, and this was the reason of their becoming so wonderfully steady and confident. Glee did most of the work with the hawks and would dash in and flush birds on a signal being given by Frost, who deserves great credit for having broken the dogs to such a high standard of steadiness and obedience.*

Alfred Frost, brother to John Frost and uncle to 'Jack', was falconer for many years to T. J. Mann of Hyde Hall, Sawbridgeworth. A capable falconer, Frost flew passage peregrines at rooks in the spring of each year in far from ideal country on the Essex/Cambridgeshire borders and at partridge in Norfolk in the autumn. The occasional merlin was flown at larks and a goshawk or two were kept. One goshawk flown for six seasons was 'Shadow of Death'. 'Vampire' and 'Valkyrie', both female goshawks also did particularly well.

George Oxer trained under John Frost as an under-falconer to the Old Hawking Club. He then went to Mr William St Quintin of Scampston Hall, Yorkshire. Serving as falconer to St Quintin until 1890, Oxer showed excellent sport at partridges and perfected gull hawking. Using mainly tiercels, both passagers and eyasses, usually flown in a cast, gull hawking proved to be of the highest class. In Oxer's last season with St Quintin the hawks took forty-three gulls in seventy-seven flights.

On the death of John Frost, George Oxer returned to the Old Hawking Club as head falconer. Charles Frost, elder brother to 'Jack', replaced him as falconer to St Quintin. Even today George Oxer is remembered locally in Wiltshire. A kindly character, he was called 'Father' George by the children and Mr G. F. Lewis, whose father had kept The Crown at Everleigh, remembers him well in his green jacket with hawk on fist.

The headquarters of the Club was at Church House, Shrewton, where the Club members repaired in March and April for the annual rook hawking, but they also used The George at Amesbury and The Crown.

136

Mr Lewis remarked on how the quiet of the Wiltshire villages was disturbed by the arrival of the Club members with horses, grooms and menservants. He remembers two assistant falconers, Bob Slightman and Ben Besent, and how a local man, Tom Salisbury, drove the covered hawk van, pulled by Jumble, that was used to convey the waiting hawks, protected from the cold winds and rain of Salisbury Plain in the early spring.

As with other falconers who served the Old Hawking Club so well, Oxer was equally at home with passage hawk or eyass. Whether rook hawking in the spring, partridge hawking at Avebury with Charles Garnett, or at Lord Sefton's in Lancashire, both members of the Club, magpie hawking in Ireland or journeying to Valkenswaard to collect the fresh-taken passage hawks for that year, a successful falconer and a kindly friend and companion to all that knew him, George Oxer will be remembered in the annals of falconry.

James Rutford, falconer to Major Fisher, was trained by John Pells at Lakenheath. Fisher having himself learnt some of the skills of falconry from Pells, it was natural that he should send his man to be tutored by the same able falconer. For more than twenty years Rutford, sometimes assisted by his brother William, served as falconer to Fisher and, outliving his master, he attended his funeral, bearing on his glove a favourite falcon, in silent testimony of the sport Fisher had loved so well.

About 1889 Major Charles Radclyffe sent Thomas Allen to be trained as a falconer by James Rutford. Tom Allen also spent a season with John Frost of the Old Hawking Club and from them learnt the rudiments of falconry and the daily management of hawks. Returning to Dorset, he

Richard Best as a loader.

James Rutford and Thomas Allen, feeding up the hawks at the end of the day.

right to left: James Rutford, falconer,
Richard Best, falconer, Tom Allen, falconer,
Gilbert Blaine, C. E. Radclyffe and Vivia
Radclyffe holding Blaine's tiercel, 'Ready'

was head falconer to Major Radclyffe for many years and during this time was in charge of what was said to be the largest establishment of trained hawks in England – partridge hawking on the heathland around Wareham, grouse hawking in Northumberland, even flying hawks as far afield as Germany and Hungary and taking part at the International Falconry Contest at Spa.

Tom Allen, in turn, trained further falconers, perhaps the best known being Richard Best, falconer for a short time to Prince Odescalchi, at Thuzer in Hungary, falconer to Captain Gilbert Blaine and falconer to the Old Hawking Club after Oxer retired at the outbreak of the First World War until the closure of the Club in 1927. Other falconers who trained under the careful guidance of Tom Allen were Fred Lightfoot who also went to Prince Odescalchi in Hungary, and W. Coleman who visited Riddlehamhope with Radclyffe and Fisher in 1897. Thomas Allen was probably the last of the old-time professional falconers. He died in Dorset in 1942.

Richard Best, head falconer to 'Guy' Blaine for more than twenty-five years, was formerly a gamekeeper to Major Radclyffe at Hyde. Trained by Tom Allen in 1897-98, he acted as falconer to Blaine who had started hawking partridge in conjunction with Major Radclyffe on his Dorset estate. During Best's first season as Blaine's falconer, with James Rutford to aid him, the hawks took a total of 102 partridge and ten sundries, by far the best work being done by two of Blaine's tiercels, 'Ready', a passage tiercel of one year, and 'Lucifer', an eyass tiercel. The following season Blaine acquired his first peregrine from Lundy. This tiercel proved to be all that was expected of him, and killed fifty-six partridges in his first season.

While with Captain Blaine, there is no doubt that Richard Best, and later his assistant Ted Woods, saw the very best of game hawking, both at partridge in Wiltshire and after 1911 at grouse in Caithness. In Wiltshire merlins were also flown with success and usually Best had a goshawk or two in hand. Later, from 1918 till 1927, Best was also responsible for the rook hawks of the Old Hawking Club.

Best's experiences were not restricted to the British Isles. In October, 1901 he and Lightfoot went to Hungary with a team of seven peregrines and a goshawk. Although rather late in the season they caught a good bag of partridge and in the spring of 1902 enjoyed first-class magpie hawking. The proud possessor of this large hawking establishment was Prince Zoard Odescalchi. Enthusiastically he sent out men in the spring of that year to obtain eyasses locally. They succeeded in getting both peregrines and sakers. A local man was trained as an additional falconer. How the two Dorset men managed the language is not recorded, but they took the field for the partridge season of 1902 with three eyass tiercel peregrines, two falcons and a female saker. As Best remarked to Major Radclyffe, who visited there in the late autumn, 'Six hawks on the cadge today and not a bad one in the lot'. All good game hawks, perfect flyers and high mounters, in a little over the first three weeks of the season they had taken over eighty partridges. The total mews consisted of fourteen peregrines, three sakers and two hobbies. They presumably had lost the goshawk they had taken with them from England.

Prince Z. Odescalchi at target practice with duelling pistols

Working for a Hungarian Prince had certain drawbacks for, although the Prince was one of the finest rifle and pistol shots of his time, he took a delight in shooting the ash off a cigar at twenty paces, the cigar held in the mouth of Richard Best. Time after time the Prince could hit coins thrown into the air, with either pistol or rifle. He was also renowned as a swordsman, all of great value in a country where duels were still the gentlemanly way to settle a disagreement.

Hawking in Hungary was certainly done in style in those days. At luncheon, a feast in itself, however far out in the country, a band would play gypsy music to entertain the guests who followed the hawking in a carriage drawn by a team of milk white horses.

Up to 1911 Richard Best continued to travel to Hungary to help Lightfoot, who remained as falconer-in-chief, but he returned for the partridge hawking at Tilshead on the Plain as falconer to Blaine. Continuing to get eyass peregrines from Lundy, Blaine and Best made first-class game hawks of nearly all of them. Now well established on good partridge ground around Tilshead and Shrewton on Salisbury Plain, the sport was of the very best. Each season they seemed to do better than the previous one. In 1911 the team consisted of two Lundy tiercels, a passage tiercel, 'Gnome', and a passage falcon, 'Antoinette'. These hawks took a total of 313 partridge, the highest score being eighty-three, the lowest seventy-two head. The following season a total of 340 partridge were taken by the hawks. While hawking on the Plain they also flew a few merlins in the early part of the season. In 1908 a total of 178 skylarks were taken with three merlins. The only goshawk of note during this period was 'Mrs Gibson' who took 134 rabbits and other various in the winter of 1906.

In 1912 Captain Blaine took the sporting rights on some grouse moors in northern Caithness. Best hacked the eyass peregrines of that year at Tilshead, then journeyed north, arriving at Barrogill Lodge on 2 August with eight peregrines, six of which were Lundy hawks, both falcons and tiercels. They finished the season with 244 grouse, an indication of the skills of both master and man. For four seasons hawks were flown over Barrogill and the surrounding moors. In 1913 over 400 grouse were taken. The following season promised to be even better but the war intervened, and, with Blaine away in London, Best continued to fly the

Richard Best, falconer to Blaine for more than 25 years

Richard Best carrying the cadge on Wool
Heath, Dorset, in 1899

grouse hawks. He enjoyed good sport and recaptured a young Lundy
tiercel Blaine had turned loose. On 8 September, when Best was flying
'Barbara', the released tiercel came up with a wild falcon, and, a covey
being flushed, all three hawks pursued and caught a grouse. On the 10th
Best caught up this tiercel as he was reported to be killing grouse on Mrs
Sinclair's moor. In 1915 Best went up to Barrogill with some of the old
hawks and a very fine passage falcon sent to Blaine by the Old Hawking
Club. This hawk, although hard in moult, proved to be as perfect a
grouse hawk as could be found.

After the war, in the autumn of 1919, Best flew two eyass falcons at
partridge on the downs near Tilshead in Wiltshire. One of these, an
Orkney falcon, showed promise as a game hawk and so, in 1920, a start
was made at grouse once again. Now at Camster Lodge in Caithness, the
grouse hawking was as good as ever but now that Blaine had taken over as
manager and secretary of the Old Hawking Club and Richard Best as

140

Club falconer, they had the opportunity to select likely passage falcons to try at grouse. Gull hawking also occupied them in Caithness and after another record year in 1922 with 406 grouse in the bag they only flew gulls when grouse were almost wiped out the following season. Grouse numbers began to improve again in 1924, and Blaine with his partner, Ken Palmer, recommenced grouse hawking, Best still being in charge of the mews, and his assistant, Ted Woods, now employed by Palmer.

At about this time the use of horses to follow the rook hawking on the Plain became impractical due to the encroachment of military training areas and the increased use of barbed wire. Army camps such as Larkhill and Bulford spread, a vast city of tin houses over much of what was once the wildest part of the plain, and ranges covered most of the downland between Lavington and Stonehenge. The Bustard Inn, where Major Hawkins Fisher and Cecil Duncombe had stayed in 1863, hawking rooks with Robert Barr as falconer, was no more a wild and secret place. Unable to follow the course of their falcons, they were lost and so the Old Hawking Club came to an end in 1926.

Richard Best retired to live at Camberley and there was employed for a short time as Club falconer to the newly formed British Falconers' Club. At a meeting held on 13 November, 1928, it was proposed that Best should be employed and this was agreed to. He died on the first of March, 1929.

Ted Woods, assistant falconer to Richard Best while working for Blaine

11
Famous Hawks

As there are celebrated falconers of the past, so there are famous and celebrated hawks and falcons. Indeed without there having been hawks and falcons whose exploits and achievements caused comment and surprise by their excellence, few, if any, of the falconers of the past would have been remembered. By no means were all the hawks owned or trained by celebrated falconers worthy of note. Falconers throughout the ages have had failures as well as successes, but brilliant hawks make great falconers, or perhaps clever falconers can produce the very best from the hawks that pass through their hands.

Falconry is not a sport of huge bags and large scores. But success in the field at quarry is one measure of the excellence of a hawk and perhaps the only way by which one can record the exploits and achievements, so making a hawk famous. Chance, of course, plays a large part in success in the hawking field. Success breeds success and, for instance, in a good grouse year, when the pointer or setter finds grouse after grouse in quick succession, then the chances of a peregrine quickly learning to wait on high steadily and to kill a large bag of grouse is very much easier. So are great hawks made.

In the early days at Didlington many fine hawks were trained, but although we have the names of some of the more successful of them, their successes in the field are not recorded. One of the earliest hawks that we can identify with a score at quarry is a peregrine tiercel, 'The General', the property of the Marquess of Carmarthen. In 1832 this intermewed eyass tiercel killed 123 partridges and six woodcock, a total of 129 head in 134 flights. This fine score at partridge does not appear to have been bettered until 1921.

Of heron hawks, three in particular have been written of as particularly successful. Herons were flown on passage, while flying out to feed or returning to their heronry, usually by a cast or pair of peregrines. Some hawks will not tolerate a companion and will 'crab', or fight, with another hawk. The most successful casts were those that regularly flew together, were tolerant of one another, and worked as a team. Such a cast were the two famous falcons, 'Sultan' and 'De Ruyter'. Both taken as passage falcons, they at first belonged to the Loo Club. They then became the property of Mr Newcome. In 1843 this successful cast took fifty-four herons and again in 1844 a total of fifty-seven herons. Each season before

(opposite) 'Dawn', a haggard falcon, trapped at Valkenswaard in 1920. In the spring of 1921 she took 57 rooks and that autumn 33 gulls and 12 grouse

'Lundy III', an eyass peregrine tiercel, 1907-14. The property of Gilbert Blaine, he accounted for 373 partridge, 106 grouse and 31 various in his eight seasons

the start of the heron hawking these falcons were flown at rooks and 'De Ruyter' was eventually lost after a rook at Feltwell. Occasionally a falcon would be found who could take heron unaided by a second hawk. Such a falcon was 'The Bull-Dog', a passage falcon taken in the nets in 1843. Owned by the Loo Hawking Club, she was equally famous for rarely needing to make more than three stoops at any heron. Newcome regarded 'Bull-Dog' as the best heron hawk he had seen.

In 1845 William Barr Senior trained an eyass tiercel which he named 'Wee Pet'. This tiercel lived about Barr's home in perfect liberty, at almost permanent hack, but would wait on, following Barr and his dog, and killed a great variety of quarry including grouse, partridge, pheasants, greyhens, snipe, peewits, skylarks and crows. Barr flew him for five seasons. Another fine tiercel at about this time was 'The Bishop'.

When the Loo Club ended in Holland, falconers turned their attentions to rook hawking as the flight most suited to the passage peregrine. In 1864 the Old Hawking Club came into being, the principal sport being the spring rook hawking. Many fine falcons and the

'Lady Jane', a passage peregrine falcon, 1920-25. She accounted for 66 rooks, 235 grouse and 2 snipe in her career

occasional tiercel were trained for this quarry during the 'reign' of the Old Hawking Club. One such was an eyass tiercel, 'Druid', who, entered at magpies in 1864, was then flown at rooks for three seasons alongside the best of the passage falcons. For an eyass tiercel to regularly handle so tough a quarry is rare, although as early as 1838 Mr Newcome had a tiercel named 'Will-o'-the-Wisp' who was equally excellent at rooks, but he was a passage hawk. For a long time the largest score at rooks for one season was held by a falcon called 'Empress'; this was in 1872 with a total of sixty-three to her own foot. Not until 1913 did a hawk better this when a passage falcon, 'Aimwell', took a total of seventy-two rooks. Another passage falcon of note was 'Bois-le-Duc'. Difficult to enter to the sable quarry, once started she killed sixty rooks in sixty-one flights. For five seasons she flew rooks each spring on the Plain and in three of those years she headed the list with the top score.

During the sixty-two years of the club's existence many hawks were trained. Each year eight or so passage hawks would be collected from Valkenswaard and many eyasses were hacked and trained at Lyndhurst. Of these some at least have been remembered. A passage falcon, 'Elsa', entered in 1886 to rooks, killed the highest score that season and continued to do so for a further two seasons. Still continuing to fly rooks each spring, she was entered to grouse in the autumn of 1887 and was eventually lost in Caithness in 1891. For a hawk to be successful at such totally different flights is not common. Two passage tiercels, 'The Earl' and 'The Doctor', trained in 1873, must be remembered as the only trained hawks that took peewits in the spring of the year.

Of eyass falcons perhaps the best known is 'Parachute', trained in 1880. A steady high-mounting falcon, she took a total of 146 head of quarry in her third season, of which fifty-seven were grouse and seventy-six partridges. In that year 100 brace of grouse were killed by hawks of the Old Hawking Club between 12 August and 14 September, on Achinduich moor, six miles north of Bonar Bridge in Sutherland. 'Vesta', a very good game falcon, from the ancient eyrie at Culvercliff in the Isle of Wight, served the Club for nine seasons. During that time she took a total of 297 grouse and forty-one various. During her first few seasons she was excellent but was rather self-willed towards the end.

Eyass tiercels such as 'Buccaneer', 'Meteor', 'Shamrock' and 'Shillelagh' all made their mark at magpie or partridge. In 1879 'Buccaneer' and 'Meteor', flown in a cast, killed forty-four magpies in thirteen days. Another tiercel of renown was 'Persimmon', an eyass tiercel from Donegal in 1897. He flew grouse each season until 1900. In one season he took seventy grouse, a record not to be broken until 1922.

To return to rook hawks, 'Josephine', another good passage hawk, killed a total of 185 rooks, but was lost half way through her fourth season. Perhaps one of the most consistent of hawks was 'Danceaway'. Caught in 1893, she took 288 rooks spread fairly evenly over seven consecutive seasons. 'Shelagh', a haggard falcon trapped in 1902, proved perfect for rooks, killing fifty-four in her first season and sixty-two in her second. She was unfortunately lost in her third season through unsound jesses.

It has always been said of haggards, because of their wild experience

often of some years duration, that they are easy to train but shifty and unreliable to fly. But the occasional haggard, such as 'Shelagh' or 'Dawn', are the exception to the rule and are pearls beyond price. 'Dawn', a haggard taken in the autumn of 1920, killed fifty-seven rooks in her first season. Taken to Scotland to be tried at grouse, she took twelve, then changing her attention to gulls she took thirty-three of these single-handed. Captain Blaine, then manager of the Old Hawking Club, reports of her: 'Dawn', *although her career lasted for only one year, takes rank among the famous rook hawks owned by the Old Hawking Club. Very few haggards have been trained successfully in modern times. They are usually ruse, unreliable and inclined to 'check', and the knowledge gained during their wild state seems to render them prone to fly cunning.*

But a good haggard is a priceless possession. Such was 'Dawn'. *Many hawks have a great aversion to rooks, and can never be induced to fly them keenly.* 'Dawn' *took kindly to them from the first: no 'slip' was too long for her, and she would fly in all weathers. She would ring up into the sky after a strong rook, and hunt in a cramped place like a terrier.*

(opposite) 'Lundy III'

'Sibella', an eyass peregrine falcon, the property of Charles Portal.

In the autumn of 1921 she was flown at gulls in Caithness. One notable gull flight is worthy of record. Slipped at a young herring gull, she bound to it at the first stoop, but in the fall she let go her hold of it. The gull at once began to ring, with the falcon in pursuit. Both mounted at a great pace into the sky, the day being clear, with a light breeze, and disappeared into a white cloud, whence they emerged still climbing, and only visible with the aid of field glasses. The falcon, who had been below, was now on a level with the gull, but, like a good hawk, she made two more rings, and then a long beat into the wind to attain altitude, her wings moving with great rapidity.

Meanwhile the gull, feeling his powers failing, turned tail to the wind, and made off as fast as he was able. A distance of half a mile now separated the two birds. The falcon came round, and shooting across the sky like a meteor until she was over the gull, made a perpendicular stoop, driving it downwards. It was then all over with the gull; she soon bound to it, and they came tumbling down together, the gull screaming loudly, still at an immense height.

The falcon now let go the gull, and it fell from her foot diving headlong downwards, with wings inert, while she glided downwards more leisurely behind it. As the gull neared the ground, she bound to it again, and keeping uppermost, landed and killed it. In this flight both gull and hawk were going all out from start to finish. This gull would have defeated a less determined hawk. She was accidentally lost in the following winter, through escaping from the room in which she was moulting.

Yet another passage falcon of excellence was 'Ursula'. In 1891 she took fifty rooks in the spring and fifty grouse in Scotland in August and September of the same year.

One further falcon from the early days of the Old Hawking Club should be mentioned, 'Esmeralda', a passage falcon of 1876. Hooded off at a packet of rooks, she would drive them up into a bunch, then, stooping, would cut out a rook and, again stooping from the throw up, would strike down a second rook. This she did on many occasions.

'Lady Jane', caught at Valkenswaard in the autumn of 1919, belonged to Captain Blaine. This falcon was flown at rooks on the downland of Wiltshire in 1920 and 1921, and subsequently at grouse in Caithness. Like many passage hawks trained in modern times, she proved to be as good at game as she had been at rooks when a young hawk. Her style was perfect, and she was very steady and reliable in her work. She could always be relied on to 'play to the gallery', and for this reason was a great favourite with all who came to see her fly. 'Lady Jane' killed sixty-six rooks, 235 grouse and two snipe during the five years in which she was flown.

Another passage falcon of nearly the same name was 'Lady Jane Grey', the favourite falcon for more than eight seasons of Major Fisher. Fisher said of this falcon that she was the very highest mounter he had ever seen. She would sometimes rise so high that she was not only beyond the reach of human sight, but even beyond the range of good field glasses.

Another famous Lundy tiercel was the third that Captain Blaine had from the island. 'Lundy III', taken in 1907, served for eight seasons and, in a letter to **The Field** on 10 April, 1915, Blaine wrote:

Sir,

I write to record the loss, during the past winter, of my old tiercel 'Lundy III', who died in a fit in the eighth year of his career. He was a game hawk second to none, and his score of close on 500 head of quarry taken during the eight seasons in which he has

(opposite) 'Bitch II', an intermewed eyass peregrine falcon, the property of Stephen Frank

149

'Bitch II'. In 1968 she took a total of 177 grouse.

been flying – an average of over sixty per annum – has not, I believe, been equalled in the annals of modern falconry. He was a brilliant and consistent performer, and no wind in which a trained hawk could be flown was too much for him. In 1913 he killed fifty grouse on my Caithness moor, holding his own with the falcons right into October.

When first flown at grouse, after five seasons at partridges in Wiltshire, he was handicapped by their greater size and weight, and lost a good many through trying to bind to them – as had been his wont with partridges – instead of cutting them over.

I remember on one occasion, having seen him lying stunned on the ground, through his having driven too violently into a grouse, that had just taken wing again, after being knocked down. He soon learnt, however, to adapt himself to the new conditions, and, waiting on steadily over the dog, he would come out of the sky like a flash, the moment a grouse was on the wing, cutting it over neatly into the heather, before it had got well under way. Then, surging rapidly up to his pitch, he would repeat the performance a second or a third time, on the grouse being again flushed, until he judged that he had mastered it, when he would come down and bind to it on the ground.

He had that rare quality in a game hawk, of waiting on up-wind of the dog's point, regulating the distance by the strength of the wind. Thus he was always well placed for grouse that would persist in going against the wind, and often succeeded in turning them downwind, as they would otherwise have been obliged to pass directly under him. Every falconer who has flown hawks at game will appreciate the advantage of this manoeuvre.

For the last few seasons of his career he was only flown late in the afternoon, one or two flights being always reserved for him, and he never then failed to play his part well.

When grouse were wild, he was invaluable, for, on these occasions, he could be quietly slipped half a mile away from the dog's point; then, ringing up high until he could see the standing setter, he would, of his own accord, go straight over the dog, and so command the grouse that the falconer had time to approach and flush them for him.

As a young hawk he was fond of chasing wood-pigeons, killing a good many, and was often lost, and left out for the night, owing to this habit. But latterly he never pursued them, unless, having been kept waiting on for a long time fruitlessly, he had made up his mind that no game could be found for him.

One of the pluckiest and most remarkable of his exploits was the retrieving of a partridge that had gone to ground in a rabbit hole. The tiercel, not to be defeated, followed it, and, after a few minutes spent underground, emerged panting but triumphant, one foot firmly gripping the dead partridge by the neck.

Many other instances could I relate of the feats of this gallant little hawk, but I must not occupy any more of your space, and so let this suffice. I would send you the yearly record of his score, but it is not at the time available.

Gilbert Blaine

Record of 'Lundy III's' score, 1907-1914

	Partridges	Grouse	Pigeons	Various
1907	59	—	—	3 small birds
1908	87	—	8	4 small birds
1909	74	—	1	4 small birds
1910	81	—	3	5 small birds
1911	69	—	—	1 landrail
1912	—	32	—	—
1913	3	53	—	1 golden plover
1914	—	21	—	1 small bird
Total	373	106	12	19 Total 510 head

Blaine had success with pretty well all the Lundy peregrines that he had over the years. 'Anna Pavlova', an eyass falcon of 1912, took sixty-one grouse in her first season, and fifty-one in 1913, her sister 'Barbara' a total of 229 grouse in four flying seasons, and 'Sylvia', an eyass of 1913, ninety grouse and three various in her first season. Again, in 1922, Blaine trained a Lundy falcon. Named 'June', she proved to be a successful and deadly grouse hawk, taking ninety-nine grouse and a blue hare in 102 flights.

Brother to 'June' was a small tiercel of outstanding excellence. Belonging to Captain Kenneth Palmer, 'Lundy I' proved equal to the best of the passage hawks at grouse. One of the very highest of mounters, he took seventy-five grouse and a snipe in his first season. On 13 September, 1922, he killed two grouse from one covey and even late into October he could cut birds down, apparently killed outright.

While Blaine was busy grouse hawking in Caithness, Charles Portal, later to become Viscount Portal of Hungerford, had started game hawking at partridge at Cranwell in Lincolnshire, and later on Salisbury Plain. In 1921 he had an outstanding tiercel peregrine named 'Rattle'. This tiercel, flown from 1 September until the end of January, took a total of 121 partridges and seven various. The following season, with an eyass falcon, 'Sibella', Charles Portal took the astonishing total of 161 partridges and four various, and in the same season had a tiercel, 'Mike', that took 111 partridge.

There is no doubt that many of these impressive scores were made in the balmy days of falconry, an era of enough time and enough money and when conditions were as near perfect as is possible. Few falconers could ever hope to exceed these individual scores, however good their hawks, under modern conditions. In these days one can only look back on the great days of falconry and of great hawks whose achievements will never be surpassed. Nevertheless in 1967 an eight-year-old intermewed eyass Scottish falcon, 'Bitch II', took a total of 101 grouse plus a snipe on two small moors in Ross and Sutherland in Scotland so carving for herself and her master, Stephen Frank, a place in the history of falconry. 'Old Bitch', not content with such success, did even better the following season by taking the extraordinary number of 177 grouse and one snipe, a 'record' that is unlikely ever to be broken.

Despite their greater size and power the gyrfalcon, or jerkin, do not feature in the lists of successful falcons in the field, at least very little since the days of kite hawking. Only one such is worthy of note, 'Adrian', a haggard jerkin taken in the nets at Valkenswaard and carefully trained for the Old Hawking Club by John Frost. Lascelles wrote of this jerkin that he was perfect in style and one of the grandest flyers the club ever possessed. But with warmer weather the hawk lost his form and was lost during his first moult.

Of merlins and their successes at skylarks much has been written, but of actual scores and names of hawks we have to wait until E. B. Mitchell and his **Art and Practise of Hawking**, published in 1900. In his chapter on lark hawking he reports that the most he has known to be killed in one season by a single merlin was in 1897 when 'Jubilee' scored 106. But, according to Mitchell, 'Jubilee' was not as good as her sister, 'Queen', who in the same season killed ninety-five skylarks. In 1883 a score of sixty-five larks was achieved by a merlin named 'Eva', who in Mitchell's opinion was the best merlin he ever had. Captain Blaine's best merlin seems to have been a jack, which killed eighty-five larks in 1908. But all these scores were bettered by 'Squeak' and 'June', two merlins belonging to Charles Portal. 'Squeak', in 1922, took the impressive number of 134 larks in 158 flights, but that did not better the score of 'June' in 1921. It is said that she never refused a lark and took 162 larks between 17 July and 1 September.

Undoubtedly there have been many famous goshawks, but, as with merlins, they have not been so thoroughly recorded as have the famous peregrines of the past. In 1885 George Oxer, then falconer to Mr St Quintin in Yorkshire, took out a female goshawk one day in November and took sixteen rabbits in seventeen flights. In the same year, John Riley of Putley Court, in Herefordshire, had a fine female goshawk named

153

'Isolt'. This gos' took 110 rabbits and twenty-one various in her first season. The following season of 1886/7 she bettered her score by taking 130 rabbits and nine various. Again she did well in her third season taking seventy rabbits before she was lost on 26 December. Another successful goshawk owned by John Riley was a haggard male taken on 15 July, 1891. This hawk, flown from 9 September until 17 October, killed twenty-one partridges, three pheasants and four various. His name was 'Tostin'. Another excellent goshawk was 'Gaiety Girl', trained and flown by Arthur Newall, a member of the Old Hawking Club. In one season she took fifty-five hares, nineteen rabbits and six various.

'Shadow of Death', a female goshawk belonging to T. J. Mann, took in one season 146 head of quarry, mainly rabbits. In the winter of 1892/3 a Norwegian goshawk took 244 head, of which 220 were rabbits. Perhaps the highest score ever made by a goshawk was 340 rabbits and thirty-four various, taken by a female goshawk during the winter of 1892/3, owned by Sir Henry Boynton of Burton Agnes in Yorkshire.

Gilbert Blaine nearly always had a goshawk or two in his mews, one of the best being a female, 'Mrs Gibson', who caught 134 rabbits and twelve hares in 1906. Flown for only a few days in 1907 she killed fourteen rabbits and two hares. One more goshawk worthy of note, 'Shaya', the property of J. L. Newman, took over 200 rabbits in the winter of 1896/7. Of sparrowhawks, 'Ruby', an eyass female of 1894, trained by Mr Riley, scored 106 blackbirds and three various in her first season, an outstanding achievement.

(*opposite*) 'Mrs Gibson', a magnificent goshawk, the property of Gilbert Blaine

Hawking Records

Scores made by hawks in one season

Merlin		
1921	'June' female (eyass) (Portal of Hungerford)	17 July/1 September 162 larks

Peregrines (Game)

1832	'The General', tiercel (eyass) (The Duke of Leeds)	129 head in 134 flights (mainly partridges)
1882	'Parachute', falcon (eyass) (Old Hawking Club)	57 grouse, 76 partridge, 13 various (146 head)
1913	'Sylvia', falcon (eyass) (Blaine)	90 grouse, 3 various (93 head)
1921/2	'Rattle', tiercel (eyass) (Portal of Hungerford)	121 partridge, 7 various (128 head)
1922	'Sibella', falcon (eyass) (Portal of Hungerford)	161 partridge, 4 various (165 head)
1922	'June', falcon (eyass) (Blaine)	99 grouse, 1 hare (100 head)
1922	'Lundy', tiercel (eyass) (Blaine)	75 grouse
1967	'Bitch', falcon (eyass) (S. Frank)	101 grouse, 1 snipe (102 head)
1978	'Bitch', falcon (eyass) (S. Frank)	177 grouse, 1 snipe, 1 wheatear (179 head)

Peregrines (Rooks)

1872	'Empress', falcon (passage)	63 rooks
1913	'Aimwell', falcon (passage) (Old Hawking Club)	72 rooks

Goshawk

1892/93	Female eyass Goshawk (Sir Henry Boynton)	340 rabbits, 34 various

Glossary

Bell, s. Trained hawks normally wear bells attached to their legs to enable the falconer to find them more easily.

Bind, v. To catch hold of quarry.

Block, s. The perch used for long-winged hawks when on the lawn.

Blue hawk, s. A hawk's adult plumage.

Bolt, to fly at, v. To fly straight from the fist at quarry.

Bowse, v. To drink.

Cadge, s. Oblong frame on which hawks are carried to the field.

Cast, s. Two hawks flown together.

Crabbing, i.e. grabbing. Said of a hawk that siezes another.

Enter, v. To fly a hawk at quarry for the first time.

Eyass, s. A nesting or young hawk.

Eyrie, s. Nest of hawk.

Falcon. The female peregrine; also used for female of other long-winged hawks.

Flush, v. To spring the quarry.

Hack, flying at. A state of liberty for eyass hawks for a few weeks during which time they return for food at the hack place.

Haggard, s. A hawk caught from the wild in adult plumage.

Hood, s. Leather cap, used to blindfold the hawk, easily removed or replaced.

Intermewed, v. A hawk is said to be intermewed after moulting in captivity.

Jack, s. The male merlin.

Jerkin, s. The male gyrfalcon.

Jesses, s. Short leather straps fastened around a hawk's legs.

Mews, s. The hawk house.

Musket, s. The male of the sparrowhawk.

Passage hawk, s. A wild-caught hawk in immature plumage.

Rake, v. To rake quarry – to strike it.

Red hawk, s. A hawk's first year plumage.

Ring up, v. To rise spirally, to gain height.

Saker, v. A desert long-winged hawk; the male is called a sakeret.

Slight falcon, s. An old name for a peregrine.

Stoop, s. The dive or swoop of a hawk.

Tiercel, s. The male peregrine, sometimes used of the male goshawk.
Varvels, s. Small metal rings attached to the ends of the jesses through which the leash may be threaded.
Wait on, v. A hawk is said to wait on when she circles over the falconer or dogs, often at a great height, in expectation of quarry being flushed.
Weather, v. To place the hawks upon their perches outside to enjoy the air.
'Yarak', s. An Eastern term to describe a goshawk or sparrowhawk that is in keen hunting order.

Bibliography

Colonel T. Thornton, **A Sporting Tour through the Northern Parts of England and Great Part of the Highlands of Scotland**, 1896
J. E. Harting, **Bibliotheca Accipitraria**, Holland Press, 1964
Gerald Lascelles, **Thirty-Five Years in the New Forest**, 1915
C. E. Radclyffe, **Around the Smoking Room Fire**, 1933
The Duke of Portland, **Fifty Years and More of Sport in Scotland**, 1932
Schlegel and Wulverhorst, **Traité de Fauconnerie**, 1844-1853
Country Life and **The Field**
The Falconer, The Journal of the British Falconers' Club

Index

Numerals in italics represent illustrations.

159